REVELATION:
A PRACTICAL
COMMENTARY

Bill Coble, D.Min.

Valdese, North Carolina

Revelation: A Practical Commentary
Copyright © 2020 by Bill Coble, D. Min.

Edited by Allen King
Published by OutFlow Publishing
Valdese, North Carolina 28690
www.outflowpublishing.com

ISBN: 978-1-7329995-5-8

All scripture references are from the King James Version unless otherwise noted.
KING JAMES VERSION (KJV): KING JAMES VERSION, public domain.

Table of Contents

FORWARD

I suppose if anyone had lived next-door to Jesse and observed the raising of those several sons, you would have tried to imagine the outcomes of those young men, and the impact they would have over their lifetimes. Which would you have chosen to make the greatest contribution? Like most of us, you would have taken a few moments along the way to encourage each of them, never really knowing which of them might excel.

I met this author while pastoring the State Street Church in Greensboro, North Carolina and had an opportunity, along with many other capable men, to encourage him on his journey. Observing him over the years, it has become obvious that dedication, tenacity, and a desire to please the Master fills his heart. He and his wife Janie have impressed us all.

It has become obvious as well, that God has a giant out there in the future, and he is preparing a champion to defeat him. I am excited to see this work's completion and to see another milestone in this journey of a dear friend.

I commend to you this book, the first, from the heart of a giant killer.

Bishop Dan Carter
Senior Pastor
Eastway Church of God
Charlotte, NC

ENDORSEMENTS

"I am honored to provide this endorsement for Dr. Bill Coble. I have had the privilege of knowing Dr. Coble for over 27 years. We first met when he came to East Coast Bible College as a freshman ministerial student. During these 27 plus years, I have clearly observed that Dr. Coble's life and ministry is marked by commitment to the Christian Faith and dedication to his continuing educational pursuits. I have watched him fulfill his ministerial responsibility as a true Christian gentleman and Pastor of a church. He has successfully pursued higher education and demonstrated great academic excellence. He has done this regardless of any obstacles or struggles he has had to face. He has not allowed anything to stop him or stand his way. His life of perseverance has been a positive impact on my life, and I am honored to call him a colleague.

-Tom Tatum, D.Min.
Former Vice President of Student Services
of East Coast Bible College

"When I first met Dr. Bill Coble, he was a student at East Coast Bible College, who came with a group of students to visit my church in Lincolnton. From the very first time I met him, I was impressed with his walk with God. I'm proud to say that, over the years Dr. Coble has become like a spiritual son to me. I am proud of the man he has become; and of the husband and dad he has become; as well as the pastor he has become. A very learned man, who loves the Lord."

-Richard A. King Sr., D.Min.
Pastor, Lincolnton Church of God

"This will be an excellent compilation of the many years of study Dr. Coble has given to the analysis of the interesting and complex Book of Revelation--a must read!"

-Dan Traxler
Evangelist and Recording Artist,
former Pastor of Dr. Coble

"In this volume, Dr. Bill Coble offers a sequential examination of Revelation. Moving through each chapter of the Apocalypse, Dr. Coble engages the reader from both a pre-millennial and pre-tribulational perspective. The eschatological realities presented in this commentary will prove helpful to the student of God's Word."

-Russell A. Morris, PhD.
Pastor, Harvest Hills Church of God

"Dr. Bill Coble is one who loves the Lord with all his heart. Many have told me that he has a great heart for ministry and people. He served as the field representative for my educational foundation for several years, and sold more books for me than anyone did during his tenure. His dedication to get things done despite his challenges has been a testimony of his faithfulness to God and His call."

-George D. Voorhis, D.Min., D.Litt.
Founder and First President
of East Coast Bible College

"It is my opinion that Dr. Coble is the premiere teacher and preacher among Western North Carolina Churches of God pastors/ministers in the subject matter of apocalyptic literature, specializing in teaching of the book of the Revelation of Jesus to John. Dr. Coble teaches in such a manner that the entire church, at all levels of education and discipleship, absorbs the materials in an amalgamated manner in his/her understanding of the Biblical canon. Dr. Coble's approach is magnificently outlined in a concise and serious manner, yet it is needful and useful for the entire congregation from laymen to seasoned pastors to first-year Christians. I am proud to say that I am able to give the highest endorsement possible, without any reservation, to the work, delivery, and the person of Dr. Bill Coble."

-Rev. Aaron Powers,
Pastor, Breakthrough Community Church of God

PREFACE

In 2008, the Lord awoke me from sleep, and spoke to my heart to proclaim the urgency of His return. At the same time, as I was studying for my M.Div. at the Pentecostal Theological Seminary, I was taking Revelation for a Greek credit. These two things combined gave me a passion for eschatology or the study of last things. I began writing this then and am grateful God has allowed me to complete this work.

This book is a 12-year journey into the book of Revelation. I have written this mostly in outline format, and in a way, I feel most people can understand. May you learn to see Revelation, not as a confusing text but as a blessed text.

I dedicate this work to the Glory of God and to my family and friends over the years.

Bill Coble, D.Min.

1

INTRODUCTION TO THE BOOK OF REVELATION

One book from the New Testament that has received a lot of attention, in recent years, is the Book of Revelation. The attention received is no accident. To some, Revelation is difficult, given the nature of the book. A careful introduction will help clear some of the misconceptions.

Revelation and Theology

Revelation basically centers around one Branch of Theology which is Eschatology or the Study of Last Things. However, other elements of Theology are there as well.

- Worship- Seen particularly in Revelation 4, 5, 11, and 19-21

- Ecclesiology- The Study of the Church-
  Revelation 2-3, 11, 19, 22
- Demonology- The Study of Satan and Demons-
  Revelation 12-13
- Pneumatology- The Study of the Holy Spirit-
  Revelation 1, 4, 11, 17, 21, 22
- Soteriology- The Study of Salvation-7, 12, 14, 19, 20

Authorship

The tradition that John the apostle wrote Revelation was widely held and almost unchallenged through the second century AD. Five times the author identifies himself as John, and though the term "apostle" is never added, he appears to have been a man of stature in the churches (1:4, 9).

Nevertheless, certain differences between Revelation and the other Johannine materials in the New Testament have led some scholars to question this tradition. There are significant differences between the Greek grammar and vocabulary of Revelation and that of the Gospel and epistles of John. Furthermore, there are theological differences in emphasis and the other Johannine writings avoid the use of the author's name.

It should be noted, however, that there are also a number of remarkable similarities between Revelation and the other books traditionally associated with the apostle John (e.g., the distinctive use of terms such as "word," "lamb," and "true," and the careful development of opposing themes such as light and darkness, love and hatred, good and evil). In addition, many of the differences can be explained by the unusual circumstances surrounding this book.

Thus, the internal evidence, while problematic, need not

overrule the early and strong external testimony to the apostolic origin of this important book.

Date

Revelation was written at a time when Roman hostility to Christianity was erupting into overt persecution (1:9; 2:10, 13). Some scholars believe that the book should be given an early date, during the persecution of Christians under the emperor Nero after the AD 64 burning of Rome. They point out that the numeric value of the Hebrew letters for "Nero Caesar" adds up to 666, the number of the beast (13:18). Evidence of this sort is weak, however, and a later date near the end of the reign of the emperor Domitian (AD 81–96) is preferable for several reasons.

Second-century church tradition testifies to a later date during the reign of Domitian. Furthermore, it is thought that John moved from Jerusalem to Ephesus c. AD 67, but this would not allow John to establish an ongoing ministry in Asia during the reign of Nero.

Finally, the contents of Revelation indicate that the Asian churches had been in existence for several years, long enough to have reached a point of complacency and decline (2:4; 3:1, 15–18). Thus, it is likely that John wrote this book in AD 95 or 96. The date of his release from Patmos is unknown, but he was probably allowed to return to Ephesus after the reign of Domitian. Passages such as 1:11; 22:7, 9, 10, 18, 19 suggest that the book was completed on of Patmos before John's release.[1]

The word "revelation" means to uncover and unveil. It means to pull back a covering or a veil that is hiding something. It also means to make known something; to reveal

---

[1] Thomas, John Christopher: *The Apocalypse*, Unpublished Work, Fall, 2007

something that a person could not find out for himself. It is a revelation of truth that man could never discover for himself. This is what the book of Revelation is: it is the great revelation of Jesus Christ to His servants or followers.

Structure of the Book

When one discusses the structure of Revelation, it is important to keep in mind that the book cannot be in chronological order. Several authors in modern church history have all tried to put this book in order. Charts from Clarence Larkin, Tim Lahaye, and others, try their best to do it. While these scholars try to use these visuals to help, one thing we must learn when it comes to the structure of Revelation is that it is more circular than chronological.

What I mean, for example, is how Revelation acts by giving the reader a little material then going back and recapping the story. For instance, we are told of the coming of the Antichrist in Revelation 6:1, then he is not mentioned again until Revelation 11. Then, the rest of his conquest is described in Revelation 13.

For the Pentecostal reader, the theme of the Holy Spirit in Revelation is one of the best ways to go about its structure as seen here:

- 1:1-8 Prologue
- 1:9-3:22- In the Spirit on the Lord's Day
- 4:1-16:21- In the Spirit in Heaven
- 17:1-21:8- In the Spirit carried to the Desert
- 21:9-22:9- In the Spirit Carried to a Great High Mountain and the New Jerusalem
- 22:6-11- The Epilogue[2]

---

[2] Thomas, John Christopher. *Two Horizons Commentary: Revelation.* Grand Rapids, Michigan: Wm. B. Eerdmans Publishing Company, 2016.

What has gotten us to Revelation?

There are several things, in the New Testament, that bring us to the book of Revelation. I like to call them "Revelation preludes".

These things include the generations of the last days, recorded in Luke 17:20-36 and Matthew 24:32-38, the kingdom parables that are found in Matthew 13, and the beginning of sorrows that are found in Matthew 24:5-8.

Generations of the Last Days

In Luke 17:20-36 and Matthew 24:32-38, we have what is called, by this researcher, the generations of the last days. There is an outline here of several generations in Bible Prophecy. They are listed as follows:

- The Outpouring Generation- Luke 17:21
- The Re-gathering Generation- Matthew 24:32-34
- The Compromising Generation- Matthew 24:37-38, Luke 17:26-27
- The Perverse Generation- Luke 17:28-29
- The Rapture Generation- Luke 17:34-36

The Outpouring Generation

The first generation we find in this discussion is the outpouring generation. The reason why this is known as the outpouring generation is that Jesus states in Luke 17:21 that the Kingdom of God is within us. This term, that is translated from the Greek within you, is used in John 14:17 where Jesus says that the Holy Spirit is in us.

We all know that in the book of Acts, the Holy Spirit was poured out in Acts 2:1-4, and that has continued since the day of Pentecost. We cannot even have a discussion on the end times or the book of Revelation without the last day sign of the outpouring of the Holy Spirit, which is confirmed as that in Acts 2:17-19.

Note in the book of Revelation, there are numerous passages where the Holy Spirit is mentioned both directly and indirectly. John says he is "in the Spirit" four different times (1:10, 4:2, 17:3, and 21:10). The seven churches in Revelation 2-3 all end with "He that hath an ear, let him hear what the Spirit saith unto the churches."

The Holy Spirit is active in Revelation with empowering the two witnesses where the word power (Greek *dunamis)* is used in canonical context to Acts 1:8. Also, it is the Spirit that enters life into the two witnesses according to Revelation 11:17.

Finally, in Revelation 22:17 the phrase "The Spirit and the bride say come" indicates that the Spirit is given to encourage the anticipation of the return of Jesus, both in the rapture and second coming. This is why it is the opinion of this writer that the Holy Spirit Generation began on the day of Pentecost and is continual for today, as we need the power of the Holy Spirit to function as God's church, and to have the anticipation of his Parousia.

The Re-Gathering Generation

The second generation is the re-gathering generation. This is found in Matthew 24:32-34, with Jesus mentioning the parable of the fig tree.

Israel is often seen, in the Old Testament scripture, as either figs or a fig tree. Jeremiah 24:1-8 and Hosea 9:10 both discuss this matter. In the parable of the fig tree, Jesus says that the fig tree would ripen.

It was in 1948 that Israel once again became a nation. Dr. George Voorhis, in his work *Notes on Revelation*, gives several "miracles" tied to this event including:

o *Miracle of retained identity.* Israel has retained her identity not just scripturally but historically as well. This is pointed out as being still called Israel in Revelation 7:4.

o *Miracle of survival.* Israel has survived every war thrown at them. These include the seven-day war, the six-day war, Yom Kippur war, continual terrorist attacks, threats from other countries, and more.

o *Miracle of the Hebrew language.* The fact that Israel was destroyed in 70 AD, and then began returning to the land, while keeping their language should also be considered a miracle.

o *Miracle of immigration.* The return of the Jewish people to their homeland.

o *Miracle of development.* The development of the land into one of the most economically stable areas of the world.[3]

The significance in the fig tree parable is also noted by the phrase "this generation shall not pass until all these things are fulfilled." This gives credence to the emphasis of the eschatological emphasis of this passage.

The Compromising Generation

The third generation to be listed here is the compromising generation. This term is given because the passages related to this generation are known as "the days of Noah". This is found in Matthew 24:37-38 and Luke 17:26-27.

To understand this passage in context, we must look back to Genesis 6.3-5. These verses record that things were being compromised. The sons of God came into the daughters of men.

---

[3] George D. Voorhis: *Notes on Revelation,* (Asheboro: Village Printing, 1988), 58-61.

In Genesis 4-5, we understand there were two lineages. The lineage of Cain, and the lineage of Seth were around during this period. One was an ungodly lineage, while the other was a Godly lineage. These two began to mix among each other, and there was wickedness and evil in the land.

The term wickedness, in the Hebrew, means violence and widespread violence. Given this language, it connects to the New Testament about the "beginning of sorrows" which will be discussed later in this writing. Further, when you consider Luke 17:26-27, you have the language suggesting everyone was having a good time and forgetting about morals.

It is interesting to note that after prayer was kicked out of American schools in 1962, and during the violence that was going on both home and abroad in the 1960's, there was an increase in drug use to escape the reality of the wickedness in the land. Truly people were using the catchphrase "if it feels good, do it."

The Perverse Generation

This carries over to our fourth generation, which is the perverse generation. This correlates to the "days of Lot" recorded in Luke 17:28-33. What stands out in this generation is how in Genesis 19, we have the destruction of Sodom and Gomorrah over open and gross sin. Just as we see homosexuality and promiscuity in this text, in the decade of the 1970's, we saw the same thing begin to take place.

In the case of Lot, we know he was living in Sodom at the time of the judgment that was getting ready to take place. Jude verse 7 also mentions Sodom, and Peter mentions Sodom's judgment in 2 Peter 2:6. Sodom is again mentioned, in Revelation 11:7-8. There is no doubt that Sodom symbolizes judgment for open and gross sin.

Worldwide, in countries such as New Zeeland, Ireland,

and other areas, homosexuality is being accepted as the norm. We have seen the trend go from tolerance to acceptance, from civil union to gay marriage, and from gay marriage to marriage equality.

The Rapture Generation

The final generation listed is what I would like to call the rapture generation. Prominent scriptures include Matthew 24:40-42 and Luke 17:35-36.

Why do I call this the rapture generation? Because now that we have seen other prophecies being fulfilled, we are one step closer to the rapture of the church.

The word rapture means to be caught up. The term rapture is not in the Bible but the meaning of it is. The meaning is used in 1 Thessalonians 4:16-17, where we are "caught up" to meet the Lord in the air, and in Revelation 4:1 where John is told "come up hither".

It would be wise here to consider that there are many views to the rapture of the church. These views include:

1) Pre-Tribulation View which teaches the rapture before the tribulation,

2) Mid-Tribulation View which teaches the rapture in the middle of the tribulation,

3) Pre-Wrath View which teaches the rapture before the last seven vials or bowls of God's wrath,

4) Post- Tribulation View which teaches the rapture at the end of the tribulation, and

5) Partial which teaches only those watching and waiting for Christ will go in the rapture.

For years, I struggled with which view to take. However, I have learned some things that have helped me decide to lean toward a Pre-Tribulation view.

The first thing I learned was, after my research looking at the Greek text, there are at least four scriptures that support a Pre-Tribulation rapture. They are Revelation 1:7, Revelation 1:10, Revelation 3:10, and Revelation 4:1. The term in two of those passages (1:10 and 3:10), "the voice as of a trumpet", parallels the text in 1 Thessalonians 4:16-17.

Secondly, there is the connection of the clouds in Revelation 1:7 with the texts of Acts 1:14 and Titus 2:13. These verses talk about His "appearing".

The Parables of Matthew 13

There are seven parables in Matthew 13 that stand out in relation to the study of the end-times. These also help lay the groundwork for our study in Revelation. They are the following:

1. The Parable of the Sower
2. The Parable of the Wheat and Tares
3. The Parable of the Mustard Seed
4. The Parable of the Leaven
5. The Parable of the Hidden Treasure
6. The Parable of the Pearl of Great Price
7. The Parable of the Dragnet

The Parable of the Sower

The Parable of the Sower is introduced in Matthew 13:3-8, while its explanation by Jesus can be found in Matthew 13:18-23. We understand that the sower is sowing the Word of God in the hearts of man, as is described in Matthew 13:3, and in its interpretation by Jesus in verses 18-23.

We must understand that during the day and time we are living in, one of the characteristics of the Church is that we are to sow the word. We see this as part of our missional mandate, given in Matthew 28:19, where we are told to "teach all nations"; in Mark 16:15 where we are told to "preach the Gospel to every creature"; and in Acts 2:42 where the church "continued in the Apostles doctrine". Also, Paul and other New Testament Writers instruct that the Word be taught, studied, and defended, which is found in 2 Timothy 2:15, 4:2, 1 Peter 3:15, and Jude 1:3.

Jesus listing four types of hearers of the Word:

o The Wayside Hearer- One who just casually hears the Word of God and the enemy (The Devil) comes and devours it. This is an accurate description of him as 1 Peter 5:8 proclaims him as a "roaring lion seeking whom he may devour".

o The Stony Ground Hearer- Here, the seed takes root but has no depth, as this hearer is full of emotionalism and because of a fear of hell, falls before the Lord in repentance. However, as soon as things become tiresome and the persecutions arise, the seed withers and dies. These are the ones who do not endure as we are commanded to do in scripture according to Matthew 10:22, John 16:33, and 2 Timothy 3:12.

o The Thorny Ground Hearer- Again the seed takes root, but when the world and its demise comes in, it "chokes" it. These are those who get carried away with materialism rather than the truth, as found in 1 Timothy 6:10, 2 Timothy 3, 4:10, and 1 John 2:15-17.

o The Good Ground Hearer- This is the individual that receives the Word and bears fruit, as found in John 15:8, Revelation 3:10, and other scriptures relating to the subject.[4]

Never in the history of the church have had we had so much access to the Word of God, and the going forth of the Gospel. Television, internet, newspapers, magazines,

---

[4] George D. Voorhis, The Course of this Present Age, (Asheboro: Village Printing, 1974), 14

social media, apps for phones, etc. have contributed more and more of this.

In May 1986, Moody Bible Institute reported that 98% of the world had a Bible in a translation that they could understand. In November 1992, *Christianity Today* reported that there were only 11,000 unreached groups left in hearing the Word of God.[5] So as time as progressed, we have gotten to the place that nearly all have heard the Word of God.

To counteract this, the Devil has tried to devour the Word of God as soon as it goes forth. Just as he tried to kill the Living Word Jesus, in Revelation 12:4 and Matthew 2:13, he wants to kill the Written Word as soon as it goes forth. So, we learn that through this parable there are some methods he uses including:

Doctrinal Heresy

Heresy means an opinion or way of thinking that contradicts the Bible.[6] So if the Bible is our doctrine, then heresy becomes doctrinal heresy. Doctrinal heresy is seen in the Word of God in many instances and should be avoided, as found in 2 John 1:10, 2 Timothy 4:2-4, and Jude 1:4. In today's church without and within, there are many forms of doctrinal heresy that run around today including:

-Jehovah's Witnesses which teaches there is no Trinity. They hold that Jesus is not the Son of God but was an angel specifically Michael the archangel. They teach that the Holy Spirit is actually a force, and that the 144,000 in Revelation 7 are selected from their adherents while the rest of the righteous, the "great crowd," live on earth, and must

---

[5] Donald Perkins, "Gospel Preached and Published," The Signs of the Times: How Close are We?, accessed October 5, 2016, http://www.according2prophecy.org/gospelpreached.html.

[6] Stanley M. Horton, ed., Systematic Theology, Revised ed. (Springfield, MO: Gospel Publishing House, 2007), WORDsearch CROSS e-book, 645.

obey God perfectly for 1,000 years or be annihilated.[7]

-The Mormons or the Church of Jesus Christ of Latter-Day Saints which teaches Trinity but hold that there are three separate parts. Eventually, nearly everyone goes to one of three separate heavenly "kingdoms," with some achieving godhood. Apostates and murderers go to "outer darkness."[8]

-The Word of Faith Movement which teaches a message of health and wealth. Within those confines are teachings such as because we were created in the image of God, we are own "little gods". They hold that God has made us as much like Himself as possible thus He made us the same class of being that He is Himself[9]

-The Oneness Pentecostals or Apostolics who believe that there is no Trinity, but Jesus is the Father, Son, and Holy Spirit. Among their teachings is that they are to be baptized only in the Name of Jesus, and that Jesus Himself used their terminology. The problem is they are taking verses of scripture and hanging their theology on it, rather than looking at the whole word of God in context. To consistently use Oneness Pentecostal logic, we would have to pronounce the words "in the name of Jesus" over everything we do, for Colossians 3:17 instructs us,

---

[7] Paul Carden, Christianity, Cults & Religions – Christianity, Cults & Religions Pamphlet, (Torrance, CA: Rose Publishing, 2010), WORDsearch CROSS e-book, Under: "Jehovah's Witnesses (Watchtower Bible & Tract Society)".

[8] Paul Carden, Christianity, Cults & Religions – Christianity, Cults & Religions Pamphlet, (Torrance, CA: Rose Publishing, 2010), WORDsearch CROSS e-book, Under: "Mormonism (Latter-day Saints)".

[9] Norman L. Geisler and Ron Rhodes, Correcting the Cults: Expert Responses to Their Scripture Twisting, (Grand Rapids, MI: Baker Books, 2005), WORDsearch CROSS e-book, 21.

"Whatever you do in word or deed, do all in the name of the Lord Jesus, giving thanks through Him to God the Father." Clearly the words "in the name of Jesus" are not intended as a formula.[10]

Persecution

Persecution is also something the enemy tries to use to take the Word of God out of our hearts. Biblically we see this in practically the entire New Testament such as Acts 7-8, 12, and 16. Historically, we see it in the Crusades with Islam, and in the modern day, we see it with the stripping away of religious freedom. Some of the biggest persecutors of Christianity in today's times can be seen in the following groups:

- Government
- Islam Extremists
- Atheists
- LGBT
- ACLU
- Schools and Universities

Materialism

Materialism and greed are another area where the Devil is taking the Word of God from hearts. This is seen by Jesus in Matthew 6:24. Materialism takes away from the truth that God is our source. This should come as no surprise, as with the original sin in Genesis 3 to now, he has tried to do this in the life of God's people.

---

[10] Norman L. Geisler and Ron Rhodes, Correcting the Cults: Expert Responses to Their Scripture Twisting, (Grand Rapids, MI: Baker Books, 2005), WORDsearch CROSS e-book, 197.

The Parable of the Wheat and The Tares

The parable of the wheat and the tares is found in Matthew 13:24-30 and is explained in Matthew 13:37-43. While the first parable of the sower deals with when the Word of God is sown, this one deals with the fruit of the seed.

This speaks of the men sown in the kingdom of God, which is represented by wheat, and also those who were not sown on good ground, which speaks of the tares. Just as Satan devoured the word, in the sower parable, here the enemy's seen (the devourer) planted within the wheat.

The wheat and the tares look alike, until it is time for the harvest. The kernel of the tares is black, which shows that since the devil cannot change the nature of the wheat, he counter sows the tares. However, the Word of God tells us that these tares must not and will not be separated from the wheat, until the judgment.[11]

Note what is happening here. From the time the Word of God has gone forth until now, Satan is counterfeiting the wheat by planting tares. The Word of God confirms this in many passages.

1 Timothy 4:1-4	**Philippians 3:18**
2 Timothy 4:3-4	**Revelation 2:2**
2 Thessalonians 2:3	**Revelation 2:9**
2 Timothy 3:13	**Revelation 2:14**
2 Corinthians 11:13	**Revelation 2:20**
Romans 16:17	**Revelation 3:3**

Revelation 3:18[12]

---

[11] George D. Voorhis, The Course of this Present Age, (Asheboro: Village Printing, 1974), 15

[12] George D. Voorhis, The Course of this Present Age, (Asheboro: Village Printing, 1974), 16

Fast forward throughout history, we understand that tares were sown in the wheat. According to research for my Doctoral Project, I found the following statistics in 1991-1992:

- 64% of Christians surveyed believe that the Ten Commandments are no longer relevant.
- 57% of Christians surveyed believe that the idea of sin is outdated.
- 32% of Christians surveyed believe that all good people will go to heaven regardless if they accept Christ or not.
- 65% of Christians surveyed believe that horoscopes and astrology provide answers to the future.[13]

And then we add in today's times and we find other examples.

Christianity continues to decline in the United States-- 7.2% annually over 2014-2015--while other religions have seen a 1.2% growth rate. Among these religions, Islam is the fastest growing one listed. Atheism continues to grow at a 1.5% rate.[14]

These statistics indicate how the Word being devoured has developed and contributed to the tares among the wheat, both inside and outside of Christianity.

The Parable of the Mustard Seed

This parable is found in Matthew 13:31-32. It deals with the growth of the Word of God in the last days.

During the early years of church history, people wondered

---

[13] William Coble, "Re-Establishing the Community Church" (DMin diss., Carolina Graduate School of Divinity, 2013), 75-76.

[14] Alan Cooperman, "America's Changing Religious Landscape," Pew Research Center, May 12, 2015, accessed October 10, 2016, http://www.pewforum.org/2015/05/12/americas-changing-religious-landscape/.

how in the world the mandates given in Matthew 28:19 and Mark 16:15 could be fulfilled. They also probably wondered how the words of Jesus in Matthew 24:14 could be fulfilled, that the Gospel would be preached to all nations. With the modern technology we have in the world today via internet, social media, email, etc., we can understand how this is possible now.

However, I would like to point out one key element. Note the "fowls of the air" lodged there. This includes the devil and his forces spoken of in the parable of the sower. This should not be surprising because he is identified as the Prince of the Power of the Air (Ephesians 2:2).

Note that the birds are lodging on top of the tree. This can be taken to mean several things. In the Old Testament, when God's people rebelled, they had high places built where their idolatry was committed. A lot of times when kings would come in, they would destroy everything but the high places.

Here in the New Testament, the birds sitting up, in relationship to the end times, show how Satan is going to have a time of authority against the church. We see this in the Church at Pergamos, in Revelation 2:13. We are told that Satan has a seat in that church, and in the Tribulation period Satan is given authority to make war with the Tribulation Saints in Revelation 13:7.

This has a strong application to the time we are living in now. Satan has tried his best to get a "nest" built in the Church. He is using, primarily, the compromise of the message and method of the Body of Christ.

Do you ever see bird nests? We are often encouraged by those around us not to disturb one when we see it, because it would bring discomfort to the birds in it.

This is exactly what is happening. There is an encouragement to make the church as comfortable as possible in this last day.

Political correctness has replaced the conviction of the Holy Ghost in so many settings. Now, instead of proclaiming the Savior's Gospel, we have replaced it with the social gospel. Instead of singing about the Blood of Christ, we sing about our works and self-righteousness. We no longer call sin for what it is, but rather a mistake with the mentality of "I am ok, and you are ok." As the church grows, the dissolution of the enemy grows as well.

The Parable of the Leaven

This parable is found in Matthew 13:33. Here, we find mention of the following things.

First, there is the mention of women. The role of women in Biblical prophecy is often used to show a negative role rather than positive, as it relates to the actions and events of the end times. For example, in Revelation 3, we see the reference to Jezebel in Revelation 2:20. Another example would be the whore of Babylon in Revelation 17:4-5.

The connection of this with leaven also shows the use of a negative term. Leaven in the Bible is often used to show sinful and doctrinal corruption. There are two primary examples of this usage:

- Jesus used leaven to describe the doctrine of the Pharisees and Sadducees in Matthew 16:11 and Luke 12:1.
- Paul used it to describe the compromising of Doctrine in 1 Corinthians 5:6-8 and Galatians 5:9.

The foundation of this leaven is the compromising that is going on in the world today. We see this in 1 Timothy 4:1, 2 Timothy 4:3, and 2 Timothy 3:13. We also see it in the popular false doctrines going around as well.

Paul defines this as a little leaven ruining the whole thing. This is made popular, in our day, by Religious pluralism and the trend of co-existing. We have moved from tolerance to acceptance.

The Parable of the Hidden Treasure

This parable is found in Matthew 13:44. What is interesting to note about this verse is the term *treasure*. Dr. John Walvoord, in his commentary, shows two references where Israel is referred to as a treasure in Exodus 19:5 and Psalm 135:4.[15] Dr. George Voorhis, in his study on the *Course of this Present Age,* also cites Romans 11:25 for this, as when the fullness of the Gentiles' time has come, Israel will be purchased.[16]

While these two Scholars seem in agreement, another viewpoint has also risen over this parable. This is that the treasure represents all of humankind where Christ purchased us with His work on Calvary. However, this view smacks of self-effort in obtaining that which only grace can give. It also violates the imagery of the other parables where Christ is the man. Others view the treasure, then, as representing Christ's treasured people, whom He bought and hid with Himself, in God (Col. 3:3).[17]

So, what does this parable mean to us? In following with the parables, this author believes this passage is dealing with Israel, and how as God's treasure they are hid to the world. This shows how Israel is going to be treated in the last days. In fact, we already know what they face.

---

[15] John Walvoord, Matthew: Thy Kingdom Come, (Dallas, TX: Kregel, 2008), WORDsearch CROSS e-book, 105.

[16] George D. Voorhis, The Course of this Present Age, (Asheboro: Village Printing, 1974), 20.

[17] Edward Hindson, James Borland, Mal Couch, Twenty-First Century Biblical Commentary Series – The Gospel of Matthew: The King Is Coming, (Chattanooga, TN: AMG Publishers, 2006), WORDsearch CROSS e-book, 133.

Historically, Israel and its people are not viewed by this world as a treasure. In 1948, when they became a nation, we know that they faced several historical wars. In present times, we see the ongoing threats against Israel from its neighbors, and even a cold heartedness from their allies. Even among evangelical Christians, there are those who question whether Israel is an important biblical nation today with a prophetic future.

Yet, as we trace the gospel narratives, Jesus came with a special purpose of redeeming Israel, although at the same time He reconciled the world unto Himself. It was Jesus, therefore, who sold all that He had in order to buy the treasure, Israel, and to purchase it with His own blood (Philippians 2:7–8; 1 Peter 1:18–19). During this present age, Israel is a hidden entity in the world, only to emerge at the end of the age as a major factor in the prophetic fulfillment leading up to the second coming of Christ.[18]

The Parable of the Pearl of Great Price

This parable is found in Matthew 13:45-46, and describes someone acquiring a personal possession, by selling all they have, in order to buy it. While the hidden treasure represents Israel, this represents the church.

The merchant in the parable of the pearl of great price is Christ, who comes to purchase, through His atonement, sinners who shall become fine pearls. The one pearl of great value would be the church for whom Christ gave His life— that is, all that he had.[19]

---

[18] John Walvoord, Matthew: Thy Kingdom Come, (Dallas, TX: Kregel, 2008), WORDsearch CROSS e-book, 105.

[19] Edward Hindson, James Borland, Mal Couch, Twenty-First Century Biblical Commentary Series – The Gospel of Matthew: The King Is Coming, (Chattanooga, TN: AMG Publishers, 2006), WORDsearch CROSS e-book, 133.

There are several other observations that can be made here. The pearl is formed by the introduction of the foreign body into the body of the oyster.

This can relate twofold to us. First, we are in a foreign land, and we are being formed, though in it, not of it. Second, the opposing force pressing against the pearl shows the suffering endured to become the church, as well as the suffering Christ had.

Another observation is that the church has been formed by gradual growth.

A final observation would be that the pearl is taken out of the oyster. This is symbolic of the church eventually taken out of the world by way of the rapture.[20]

The Parable of the Dragnet

This parable is found in Matthew 13:47-50. Whenever Jesus dealt with the sea, we understand that he refers to the sea of Galilee in His teachings. Because of its large character, the net collects a multitude of different kinds of fish, described in the text as "every kind." Nets of this size were too large to empty into a boat and had to be drawn to shore. Here the fish were sorted. Those that were bad, or for any reason unusable, were cast back into the sea. The good fish were gathered into the vessel.[21]

Just as this was going on in this sea, the symbolism here is interpreted as there will be a time that judgment will take place. Angels were described as separating those who are wicked from among the righteous, the wicked being described as wailing and gnashing their teeth as they were cast into the

---

[20] George D. Voorhis, The Course of this Present Age, (Asheboro: Village Printing, 1974), 21.

[21] John Walvoord, Matthew: Thy Kingdom Come, (Dallas, TX: Kregel, 2008), WORDsearch CROSS e-book, 106.

furnace of fire (Mt 13:50).

This situation is parallel to the judgment of the nations in 25:31–46. The righteous who remain after the wicked are gathered out can enter the kingdom. The general situation is the same as the separation of the wheat and the tares and their judgment, described in 13:41–43.

The fulfillment of the prophetic truth in this parable will occur at the second coming of Jesus Christ, when the world is judged, and the kingdom instituted. It is quite clear from this parable, as with those preceding, that the present age does not end in a postmillennial triumph, with the entire world being Christianized; neither does it fulfill the kingdom promises of the Old Testament nor does it describe the period when all nations will serve the Lord. Rather, as in preceding parables, it describes the dual line of good and evil, continuing until the time of the end when both the good and evil are judged according to their true character.

It is significant that the net, representing the kingdom of heaven as a sphere of profession included all kinds, both wicked and righteous, and that the separation did not come until the end. This passage serves to distinguish the kingdom of heaven from the kingdom of God which includes only the righteous. Neither the parable of the wheat and the tares nor the parable of the good and bad fish, as related to the kingdom of God, is mentioned in the other gospels.[22]

"And Jesus answered and said unto them, Take heed that no man deceive you. For many shall come in my name, saying, I am Christ; and shall deceive many. And ye shall hear of wars and rumours of wars: see that ye be not troubled: for all these things must come to pass, but the end is not yet. For nation shall rise against nation, and kingdom

---

[22] John Walvoord, Matthew: Thy Kingdom Come, (Dallas, TX: Kregel, 2008), WORDsearch CROSS e-book, 106-107.

against kingdom: and there shall be famines, and pestilences, and earthquakes, in divers places. All these are the beginning of sorrows." -Matthew 24:4-8

These verses include some of the "signs" of the last day that is often talked about in various studies.

- **Great Deception**
- **Political Unrest and War**
- **Famines**
- **Pestilences or Sicknesses**
- **Earthquakes in Diverse Places**

The first sign we see listed is great deception. Jesus makes it even more clear that this specifically deals with those who come claiming they are Him (Jesus) and will deceive many. Throughout history there are several that have done this, but in recent memory two stand out.

Who can forget the 1970's and the following Jim Jones had as part of his cult during that period? There is video footage of him saying that he is God, on the documentary *The Seventies*. Then, in the 1990's, we had David Koresh and the incident in Waco, Texas with the Branch Davidian Compound.

Others besides these try to lay claim to this false teaching. The more this happens, the more we are nearing the end.

The second sign listed here, in Matthew 24, is the political unrest and war. Nation against nation and kingdom against kingdom, having wars and rumors of wars. The Greek word for against can also be translated within. This explains a lot of the conflict that is going on today in the Middle East where countries such as Iraq, Syria, Yemen, and others are ripping each other apart from within. It also explains what is going on even in our country with political parties, agendas, and other things are dividing us.

Truly this is contributing also to the apostasy we both see and are reading in scripture with parallel passages of 2 Timothy 3:1-5, 4:3-4, and 1 Timothy 4:1-5.

The third sign we see here in our text is famines. Famines are a result of war and political unrest. We have seen our share of famines from Africa and third world countries all the way to the United States. The famines we see now in the beginning of sorrows. I believe all this is laying the foundation for the Antichrist to take control of the world economy in the book of Revelation.

The fourth sign we see here is pestilences. Pestilences are often defined as diseases. In the last ten years, we have seen new types of epidemics come our way such as the bird flu, the swine flu, the H1N1 virus, and of course COVID-19, while old ones have re-emerged such as measles, small pox, and even polio.

The fifth sign is earthquakes in diverse places. This can be seen, as we are having them on a daily basis. From the mountains of North Carolina to California and Alaska, we are seeing this being fulfilled repeatedly!

Conclusion

So here we are, on the brink of the return of the Lord. With that, the words of Revelation have meaning and context. It is with this foundation we begin our journey.

2

IN THE SPIRIT
ON THE LORDS DAY:
REVELATION 1-3

Revelation 1

This is a Revelation of Jesus Christ. It is to be understood, at this point we already had one revelation of Jesus. When he came the first time, but when he comes the second time it will be a different revelation.

Verse 1 makes it clear who wrote Revelation. The author is the Apostle John. He also wrote the Gospel of John and 1-3 John.

Verse 2 talks about him bearing the record of God. The Word "record" here comes from the Greek word *martureo* meaning to witness, to lay down one's life for a witness. This poses a question to the reader, in that how badly does one want a revelation of Jesus Christ in one's life today?

In verse 3, we read that there is a blessing to those who read the book of Revelation. That blessing is the receiving of a revelation of Christ.

Verse 4 talks about the seven churches, which are covered in Revelation 2-3. Verses 4-8 tell us more about Jesus and the fact He is: 1) the Faithful Witness (1 Corinthians 1:9, 10:13, 1 Thessalonians 5:24, 2 Thessalonians 3:3, and Revelation 19:11), 2) Washed us with His own blood (Matthew 26:28, Romans 3:25, Romans 5:9), Cometh in the clouds (Matthew 24:30, 26:64, Acts 1:9-11), 3) Alpha and Omega (John 1:1-4, 10:30).

In verse 9, John introduces himself as the author. John declares, to his readers here, that he is their companion in tribulation. Keep in mind that the date of the writing, 95-96 AD, was during the persecution of Domitian in the Roman Empire. The word tribulation here refers to that period of oppression and does not refer to the seven-year tribulation or any tribulation mentioned in the foregoing verses of the Apocalypse.[23]

Verse 10 records that John was "in the Spirit on the Lord's Day." The Term "in the Spirit" gives us a significant literary marker of the Book of Revelation. This is mentioned three other times (Rev 4:2; 17:3; 21:10). John's use of this phrase suggests that: 1) The Holy Spirit is active in the vision of the prophecy; and, 2) The Holy Spirit is active during the tribulation, because souls are being saved; and, the Spirit empowers the two witnesses in Revelation 11.

Also, in verse 10 there is the term "Lord's Day". There are several schools of thought about this phrase. First there is Lord's Day as being the Christian day of worship, the first day of the week, the day of Christ's resurrection (see Acts 20:7; 1 Cor 16:2). Only here in the New Testament is the expression

---

[23] Clarence J. Larkin: The Book of Revelation: Illustrated, Philadelphia, Erwin Moyer Publishers, 1919, 8

the Lord's day used, but it is found in early Christian literature: *Didache 14* (the end of the first century), and Ignatius' *Letter to the Magnesians 19* (early second century). The same adjective that is translated the Lord's is used in the phrase "the Lord's Supper" (1 Cor 11:20).[24] Second, there is the thought, which the author of this commentary leans toward, that the Lord's Day terminology used in this text is the start of the Day of the Lord. The Old Testament describes this as the events of the end times leading to the Return of Christ. The reason the author leans towards this is the usage of the voice of the trumpet which canonically is tied to 1 Thessalonians 4:16-17 with the event of the rapture. If then this is the start of the "Day of the Lord", then this is a strong argument for the pre-tribulation rapture which defined as the rapture before the tribulation period.

Another phrase in verse 10 that is eye catching is the "sound of the trumpet." God's proclamation with the trumpet should not be any surprise to the reader. When one sees this term, reflection can be made to several past instances in the Word of God. A trumpet in the Old Testament was often a ram's horn. But here it signifies a sound God used to break His silence.

We see several examples of this including Mt. Sinai- "voice of a trumpet, exceedingly loud", Services of Worship- began with a trumpet, and the Year of Jubilee- began with the sound of a trumpet.[25] In the New Testament, we have the trump of God, in 1 Thessalonians 4:16-17, and the trumpet used with the resurrection in 1 Corinthians 15:52. From these first ten verses in the Apocalypse, one can see that the trumpet means life, warning, and resurrection.

---

[24] (From the UBS New Testament Handbook Series. Copyright © 1961-1997, by United Bible Societies.)

[25] From The Apocalypse: Exposition of the Book of Revelation, Electronic Database. Copyright © 1998, 2003, 2006 by Biblesoft, Inc. All rights reserved.)

There are two things that stand out in this stretch of text, in verses 11-16. These are emphasized with the phrase "what you see write in a book". First, the repeated terms of "like" and "as" show that John was writing about something he was not accustomed to. The thing that is neat is that He was present on the Mountain of Transfiguration and had a glimpse of this already (Luke 9:28-36).

Second, the term "one speaking like the son of man" in this text recalls one to Daniel 7:13. As we already discussed in the introduction and prologue, Daniel plays a part in the language of the Book of Revelation.[26]

Jesus makes three statements, in verses 17-18. First, Jesus says that He is the "First and the Last", which is a repeat of what He said in verse 8. Second, He says that He "lives and was dead" which shows the atonement of Jesus Christ, and the resurrection that follows. Third, He says He has the "keys of death and hell". This identifies the vision of verse 17, which is a glorified Jesus that is coming again.

In verse 19, we have a basic structure of the book. First, there are the "things which thou hast seen" which is covered in Revelation 1. Second, there are the "things which are" that is covered in Revelation 2-3, and then the "things which shall be hereafter" which is covered in Revelation 4-22. Finally, in verse 20, the symbolism of Revelation is explained.

Revelation 2-3

Revelation chapters two and three deal with the Seven Churches of Asia Minor. There are many views to the way the reader looks at these Seven Churches. For one, the reader may approach this part of Revelation as viewing the Seven Churches as separate dispensations of history. For instance,

---

[26] Craig R. Koester: *Revelation and the End of All Things, Grand Rapids, Eerdman's, 2001*

each church represents each period of history as we know it. Another way one may view these seven churches is to view them as from a historical perspective only. The third and final view a reader may see is that there can be some practical application from each church for us today. It is the opinion of this writer that this is the best approach to take.

Introduction

To introduce the Seven Churches, one can go to the basic structure of each of them, because they are basically the same.

- There is the salutation which gives the greeting and the name of the church it is written to.
- There is an identification of Jesus in the salutation.
- There is the commendation, or a complement Jesus gives the church.
- There is the condemnation which contains a rebuke of what each church is doing wrong.
- There is the "what to do" or instruction, which usually is repent and get back on course.
- There is the promise to overcomers, which gives some element of what happens at the end to those who overcome, and the consequence to those who do not.
- There is the conclusion, or closing, which basically has the same theme of "He that hath an ear, let him hear what the Spirit saith unto the churches."

Ephesus

The first church mentioned in this stretch of text is the Church of Ephesus. Ephesus means "desirable one".

The city was a commercial and politically strong city in Asia Minor. Ephesus laid at the mouth of the Cayster River (in the country of Turkey). This river flowed fast and it tended to silt up. They would keep it clean to have a great harbor, but the Ephesians eventually lost the battle with the silt. The ruins of Ephesus are now located some six miles inland from the sea.

When people disembarked at the harbor, they traveled to the center of the city along a beautiful, wide road lined with columns. This road was called the Arcadian Way.

Three trade routes converged in Ephesus: One from the Euphrates River (East); One from Galatia (Asia Minor); One from the Maender Valley (South). This city had an active business climate with a population at this time of one quarter to a half a million people.

The city had the title of Supreme Metropolis of Asia. It was a free, self-governed city in the Roman Empire. There were no Roman troops stationed here. When a Roman governor entered Asia, he, by law, had to enter Asia through Ephesus. Ephesus was considered an assize town which made it an important judicial center. The Roman governors would try important cases in these towns; Ephesus being one of them. Ephesus was familiar with the pomp and splendor of Rome when these governors would arrive at the city.

Ephesus was also the center for the Panamanian Games which were ranked with the Olympic Games. These games were held in the month of May. The Greeks called this month Artemesion, the month sacred to Artemis or Diana.[27]

In the salutation, Jesus is introduced as the one who holds the seven stars in His right hand, and the one who is amid the seven golden candlesticks. Christ's description of Himself in this letter emphasizes two things. First, He holds the seven stars. Christ has absolute authority over the messengers to the churches. He places them in the church; He is the Author of

---

[27] Rod Mattoon, Mattoon's Treasures – Treasures from Revelation, (Springfield, IL: Lincoln Land Baptist Church, n.d.), WORDsearch CROSS e-book, 39-40.

the messages which they deliver. He keeps them in the churches or removes them from the churches. Unless His messenger is in the midst, they are not Church; they are merely human organizations.

Second, He is walking amid the seven churches. He is the all holy one, who, by His presence, sanctifies and qualifies the church, walks amid the church, seeing and rebuking its sinfulness and seeing and rewarding its good works.[28]

In the commendation, Ephesus is given three complements. Jesus mentions their labor or toil, their patience or steadfastness, their abhorrence of those who were evil, and their ready detection of false teachers, who even claimed to be apostles but who were not. These remarkable characteristics are sorely needed in the church today, where too often there is failure to serve the Lord patiently, and the tendency is to compromise both with moral and theological evil. The Ephesian church is therefore commended for abhorring that which is morally bad as well as that which is theologically in error.

In contrast to the fact that they could not bear those who were evil, he commends them for continuing to bear their proper burdens, repeating again the fact that they have patience, literally, that they "keep on having patience," which is an advance on the statement in verse 2. Likewise, it is noted that their labor is motivated as work "for my name's sake" and that they have not fainted or grown weary. These remarkable characteristics establish the fact that the church had served the Lord well, and few modern churches could qualify for such commendation.[29]

The condemnation, for Ephesus, was one of loss of first

---

[28] R. Hollils Gause, Revelation: God's Stamp of Sovereignty on History, (Cleveland, TN: Pathway Press, 1998), WORDsearch CROSS e-book, 48.

[29] John Walvoord , The Revelation of Jesus Christ, (Chicago: Moody Press, 1966), WORDsearch CROSS e-book, 55.

love. The constant lure of temptation was all around them, but they remained true to Christ. "But I have this against you," He said, "that you have left your first love" (2:4).

The church's "first love" could refer to several things: its love for Christ, the fervency of new believers, or the basic priorities of the church. As time had passed, their love had diminished. Their church life was filled with other priorities. The basics of Christian living were being neglected. So, the Lord of the Church calls them back to their original commitment to those basic priorities.[30]

The "what to do" for this church means that Christ called them to remember from whence they had fallen: "Keep on remembering the love from which you have fallen" (Rev. 2:5). The language of this call shows that the Ephesians were still in this fallen condition. To compromise one's love is a fall. It cannot be passed off as maturing, growing out of youthful zeal or any of the other excuses we offer for failing to love. Such a failing can be corrected only by repentance. A recalling of what was once true is essential to repentance. Repentance must also take the form of a renewal of those spiritual manifestations that had shown their first love.

The consequence of not repenting is drastic: "I am coming to you, and I will remove the candlestick" (2:5). The language shows that judgment is about to fall. God will not tolerate a loveless church, not even if it is doctrinally pure as this church seems to have been. If Christ removed the candlestick, this church would be without evidence of Christ's presence and without light. It would no longer be Church. The body would lose its function.

From this rebuke and call to repentance Christ returns to

---

[30] Edward Hindson, Twenty-First Century Biblical Commentary Series – The Book of Revelation: Unlocking the Future, ed. Mal Couch and Ed Hindson, (Chattanooga, TN: AMG Publishers, 2002), WORDsearch CROSS e-book, 35.

commendation. It is a commendation for doctrinal purity: "You hate the works of the Nicolaitans, which I also hate" (2:6).

The references found in Revelation 2:14, 15 and 2:20-23 show that the doctrine of the Nicolaitans, the error of Balaam and the scene attributed to Jezebel are all related.[31]

The promise to overcomers in this section is one of invitation and promise. It starts as the others do with "He that has an ear let him hear what the Spirit says unto the churches" which shows the Holy Spirit is active in God's church. However, the promise to overcomers here is that "To him that overcometh will I give to eat of the tree of life, which is in the midst of the paradise of God." The promise, mentioned here for overcomers, is not a message to a special group of Christians distinguished by their spirituality and power in contrast to genuine Christians who lack these qualities; it is rather a general description of that which is normal, to be expected among those who are true followers of the Lord. The Apostle John in his first epistle asks, "Who is he that overcometh the world?" (I John 5:5). He answers the question, "He that believeth that Jesus is the Son of God." In other words, those in the Ephesian church who were genuine Christians and by this token had overcome the unbelief and sin of the world are promised the right to the tree of life which is in the midst of the paradise of God.

This tree, first mentioned in the Garden of Eden in Genesis 3:22, is later found in the midst of the street of the new Jerusalem, where it bears its fruit for the abundant health and life of the nation (Rev. 22:2). It is especially appropriate that those who hate the evil deeds of the world and the idolatrous wicked worship are given that spiritual recompense of abiding in the abundant life which is in Christ in the eternity to come.

---

[31] R. Hollils Gause, Revelation: God's Stamp of Sovereignty on History, (Cleveland, TN: Pathway Press, 1998), WORDsearch CROSS e-book, 50.

The gracious nature of the promise is designed to restore and rekindle that love of Christ known in the early fervent days of the church and to be realized without diminishing in the eternity to come.[32]

Smyrna

The second letter was addressed to Smyrna, a large and wealthy city 35 miles north of Ephesus. Like Ephesus, it was a seaport. In contrast to Ephesus, which today is a deserted ruin, Smyrna is still a large seaport with a present population of about 200,000. Christ described Himself as the First and the Last, who died and came to life again. Christ is portrayed as the eternal One (cf. 1:8, 17; 21:6; 22:13) who suffered death at the hands of His persecutors and then was resurrected from the grave (cf. 1:5). These aspects of Christ were especially relevant to the Christians at Smyrna who, like Christ in His death, were experiencing severe persecution.

The name of the city, Smyrna, means "myrrh," an ordinary perfume. It was also used in the anointing oil of the tabernacle, and in embalming dead bodies (cf. Ex. 30:23; Ps. 45:8; Song 3:6; Matt. 2:11; Mark 15:23; John 19:39). While the Christians of the church at Smyrna were experiencing the bitterness of suffering, their faithful testimony was like myrrh or sweet perfume to God.[33]

"I know your tribulation and poverty" (2:9). These words introduce Christ's commendation of the church. They labored under the "burden that crushes," being persecuted by both Jews and pagans.

---

[32] John Walvoord , The Revelation of Jesus Christ, (Chicago: Moody Press, 1966), WORDsearch CROSS e-book, 59.

[33] John Walvoord and Roy Zuck, ed., The Bible Knowledge Commentary: An Exposition of the Scriptures by Dallas Seminary Faculty, (Colorado Springs, CO: Cook Communications, 1985), WORDsearch CROSS e-book, Under: "B. The Letter to the Church in Smyrna (2:8-11)".

Their tribulation lay in their deep economical and abject poverty. It is not simply that the Smyrneans had no surplus; they had nothing at all. It is likely that the economic depression was imposed by their enemies in a refusal to employ them or to trade with them.

"But you are rich" virtually leaps off the page of Scripture to shine in brilliant contrast to the tribulation and poverty. These believers were rich in spiritual goods. Persecution and poverty cannot affect this wealth except to enhance it.

Christ did not promise to make the Smyrnans materially rich or to take away their persecutions. Instead, He said that He knew the blasphemy of the people who oppressed them. This placed the enemies under divine wrath. Their persecutors were those who called themselves Jews. They were, by racial identification and external religious practices, Jewish; and they continued to observe the Jewish worship practices and restrictions.

Christ's judgment is that they are not Jews (2:9). The Scriptures use the term "Jew" to describe those who are of the spiritual seed of Abraham: "For he is not a Jew, which is one outwardly.... But he is a Jew, which is one inwardly (Romans 2:28, 29). Spiritually these people were the very opposite of Judaism; they were the "synagogue of Satan" (Revelation 2:9). The synagogue was the gathering place for the people of God. These people had distorted their place of gathering; it had become the synagogue of the adversary—Satan.

Suffering by the people of God in Smyrna is certain and imminent. Christ puts this warning in a word of comfort: "Fear none of those things that you are about to suffer" (2:10). Christ further warns, "The devil is about to cast some of you into prison" (2:10). Satan is the immediate spiritual agent in this act against the Smyrneans. His purpose is to destroy by oppression, discouragement, and temptation.

This trial is specifically limited by the authority of Christ:

"You shall have tribulation ten days" (2:10). The number ten is symbolic of completeness. This tribulation will last for a specific period—a relatively short period—and then it will be finished.

Though Satan will inspire this trial, he cannot control it in its timing or its duration. Christ is sovereign over those afflictions that try His people. This is not the Great Tribulation.

Christ closed this prediction with an exhortation and a promise: "Keep on being faithful until death, and I will give you the crown of life" (2:10). This divine Word gives the strength to endure the affliction. As divine Word, the promise has the guarantee of God himself. It is clear from this letter that some will die in their faithfulness to God under the period of oppression predicted.

The reward of endurance is the crown of life (2:10). The word for crown (stephanos) describes the garland or laurel wreath that was used to reward winners in athletic contests. It was not a crown of royalty. It was the victor's crown. That crown was corruptible (perishable), but the crown that Christ gives is incorruptible (1 Corinthians 9:25). This word is also used for a crown of righteousness (2 Timothy 4:8) and for the crown of glory (1 Peter 5:4). James uses the word about the crown of life (James 1:12).

The crown of life is victory over death even in death. This is death without a sting, because the receiver of the crown of life will not suffer any loss at all by the second death (Revelation 2:11). This is a crown of everlasting life; therefore, the one who wears it cannot enter spiritual death. The second death is God's judgment upon those who suffer eternal damnation (20:6, 14; 21:8). Those who conquer—enduring even to the point of sacrificing their mortal life for

Christ's sake—cannot be affected by this judgment (1 Cor. 15:55-57).[34]

Pergamos

Forty miles north of Sardis sits ancient Pergamum in the Caicus Valley. Pliny, the Roman writer, called it "the most famous city in Asia." It was the center of Roman power and authority in the province. In fact, the Pergamanians worshiped power. As early as 29 b.c., it became the site of the first temple of the Caesar-cult, erected in honor of Augustus Caesar. The city also housed an ancient temple to the god Zeus—the god of power. The altar from that temple is in the Berlin Museum and was often visited by Adolf Hitler. Pergamum (also, Pergamos) was the epitome of the hunger for power in pagan society.

There was no distinction between religion and politics in Pergamum. The city's coins depicted intertwined serpents to represent the interconnection between the sacred and the secular. For the pagans in this city, politics was religion and religion was politics. And for the Christians, there was a constant temptation to compromise their beliefs and practices for political gain.

Religion has always had a precarious relationship to political power. When power is on the side of religion, it tends to corrupt it. But when power is against religion, it tends to persecute it.

Unfortunately, the pressure of persecution often drives religion to seek power as a means of protection and self-preservation. In time, religion itself often falls victim to the very thing it opposes. It has been observed, more than once,

---

[34] R. Hollils Gause, Revelation: God's Stamp of Sovereignty on History, (Cleveland, TN: Pathway Press, 1998), WORDsearch CROSS e-book, 52-54.

that the ultimate subversion of Christianity occurs whenever we confuse spiritual authority with political power.[35]

Christ began His letter to the church at Pergamum by reminding them, "I know where you dwell" (Rev. 2:13). He was fully aware that these believers were surrounded by a non-Christian society and exposed to its values, standards, and pressures. Confrontation between the power of the state and the young Christian church was inevitable.[36]

The term "Satan's seat" is not translated as throne as the word throne is seen throughout Revelation. This demonstrates the mockery of Satan with the heavenly throne of God such as the throne that is seen in Revelation 4:2.

Christian tradition claims that Gaius (3 John 1) was the first bishop of Pergamum and that he was succeeded by Antipas, whom the Lord refers to in His letter as "My witness, My faithful one" (2:13). His name (Greek, anti pas) means "against all", and may refer to his willingness to stand against all compromise and temptation.[37]

Despite commending believers for holding fast to the faith (2:13), Christ had a few complaints against this church, in Pergamum. Apparently, some in the church were tolerating those who were teaching or practicing what Christ opposed. Christ described the church as tolerating some believers who were like Balaam, who had shown Balak how to trip up the people of Israel. Balaam had done that, in a roundabout way,

---

[35] Edward Hindson, Twenty-First Century Biblical Commentary Series – The Book of Revelation: Unlocking the Future, ed. Mal Couch and Ed Hindson, (Chattanooga, TN: AMG Publishers, 2002), WORDsearch CROSS e-book, 37-38.

[36] Edward Hindson, Twenty-First Century Biblical Commentary Series – The Book of Revelation: Unlocking the Future, ed. Mal Couch and Ed Hindson, (Chattanooga, TN: AMG Publishers, 2002), WORDsearch CROSS e-book, 38.

[37] Ibid., 38

by influencing some in Israel to worship idols by eating food offered to idols and by committing sexual sin.

The complete story of Balak and Balaam is recorded in Numbers 22–25. In brief, Balak was a king who feared the large number of Israelites traveling through his country, so he hired Balaam, a sorcerer, and told him to pronounce a curse on them. Balaam had refused at first, but an offer of money had changed his mind. Numbers 25:1-3 describes the Israelite men getting involved with pagan women and then worshiping the gods of Moab. While these verses do not mention Balaam, Numbers 31:16 explains that Balaam knew he could undermine Israel's worship and power by sending the Moabite women to entice the men of Israel. Balaam's influence caused great disaster for Israel, and he has earned the station as one who led people astray (see 2 Peter 2:15: Jude 1:11).

The church in Pergamum had stood strong against persecution, but what Satan could not accomplish from without, he was trying to do from within—through a Balaam-like deceit. Christ rebuked the church for tolerating those who, like Balaam, were undermining people's faith. Apparently, some in the church were corrupting others in their attempt to justify idol worship—perhaps by joining in with civic ceremonies where idols were worshiped. Eating food offered to idols probably refers to these people's taking part in pagan feasts. The sexual sin mentioned here may also be understood as being part of certain pagan festivities.

The church also had some Nicolaitans among them— people who follow the same teaching and commit the same sins as those who were like Balaam. These two groups were essentially the same in their practices. The Nicolaitans are described, in Revelation 2:6, as those whose actions Christ hates. The believers in Ephesus had recognized the error of these people, but apparently the believers in Pergamum were being deceived by it. The Nicolaitans were Christians who had compromised their faith to enjoy the sinful pleasures of their society. But such compromise could only dilute their faith; thus, Christ said it could not be tolerated.[38]

Christ sharply rebuked the church with the abrupt command, Repent therefore! They were warned, Otherwise, I will soon come to you and will fight against them with the sword of My mouth. He promised that the judgment would come "soon" (tachys) which also means "suddenly" (cf. 1:1; 22:7, 12, 20). Christ would contend with them, using the sword of His mouth (cf. 1:16; 2:12; 19:15, 21). This again is the Word of God sharply judging all compromise and sin.[39]

Once again, the promise to the overcomers starts with "He that hath an ear, let him hear what the Spirit saith unto the churches."

We must pay attention and respond to the warnings of the Holy Spirit today. He continues to speak the same words Jesus spoke to the seven churches of Asia, commanding us to stay true to God's Word, overcome sin in the world and not to tolerate immoral behavior among the people of God. If we lose our victory in these important areas, we lose God's favor, his guiding presence and the Holy Spirit's power. In the end, we will become enemies of God's kingdom. But there is continued promise of help for those who remain faithful and depend completely on God to help them overcome. These are the ones who receive the hidden manna (cf. Ps 78:24; see Jn 6:48-51, 58, 63), which means spiritual life, nourishment, and fulfillment from a personal relationship with Jesus Christ. We will also receive a "white stone," which represents the triumph

---

[38] Barton B. Bruce et al., Life Application New Testament Commentary, (Wheaton, IL: Tyndale House, 2001), WORDsearch CROSS e-book, 1212-1213.

[39] John Walvoord and Roy Zuck, ed., The Bible Knowledge Commentary: An Exposition of the Scriptures by Dallas Seminary Faculty, (Colorado Springs, CO: Cook Communications, 1985), WORDsearch CROSS e-book, Under: "4. Exhortation (2:16)".

of our faith over everything that was aimed at destroying our devotion to Christ.[40]

This letter to Pergamos gives us several conclusive observations:

First, there is the love for the truth. We cannot tolerate doctrinal error under the excuse that we must love everybody. First and foremost, we must love the truth and let it be the final authority in the church.

Secondly, there is the desire for holiness. We cannot win a lost world with a worldly Christianity. Only godly believers who practice what they preach will win them to Christ. Integrity is the missing ingredient in modern religion. The unbelieving world will not listen to anyone who does not have it.

Third, there is willingness to repent. The Lord called upon this church to repent of their compromise. If He insisted, they repent, how much more would He call upon us to do the same! To those who would repent, He promised three things: 1) hidden manna, 2) a white stone, 3) a new name. All three of these point to His high priestly role. The manna was hidden in the Ark of the Covenant (Ex. 16:32-34; Heb. 9:4). The white stone was the Urim on the high priest's vestment. And the "new" name was the self-revelation of Christ (cf. Rev. 3:12,).[41]

Thyatira

The fourth message of Christ was addressed to the angel of the church in Thyatira, a small thriving town located about

---

[40] Donald C. Stamps and J. Wesley Adams, ed., Fire Bible, (Springfield, MO: Life Publishers International, 2009), WORDsearch CROSS e-book, Under: "Study Notes".

[41] Edward Hindson, Twenty-First Century Biblical Commentary Series – The Book of Revelation: Unlocking the Future, ed. Mal Couch and Ed Hindson, (Chattanooga, TN: AMG Publishers, 2002), WORDsearch CROSS e-book, 39.

forty miles southeast of Pergamos. This city had been established as a Macedonian colony by Alexander the Great after the destruction of the Persian empire.

Located in a rich agricultural area, Thyatira was famous for the manufacture of purple dye. Numerous references are found, in secular literature of the period, to the trade guilds which manufactured cloth.

It is remarkable that Christ should single out a small church in a relatively obscure city for such an important letter. However, the message reaches far beyond the immediate circumstances in the church at Thyatira. One other mention of Thyatira is found in Acts 16:14–15 where the conversion of Lydia is recorded in these words: "And a certain woman named   Lydia, a seller of purple, of the city of Thyatira, which worshipped God, heard us: whose heart the Lord opened, that she attended unto the things which were spoken of Paul."

As there is no record in Scripture of any evangelistic effort in the city of Thyatira, it may be that the gospel was first brought to Thyatira through the instrumentality of Lydia. Her role of a seller of purple indicates that she was a representative of the thriving trade in purple cloth originating in Thyatira. Though Lydia was probably already deceased, Christ directed the longest of the seven letters to this small Christian assembly which may have been the fruit of her witness. All was not well in Thyatira, and to this little church is addressed one of the most severe of the seven epistles.[42]

Jesus describes Himself, in the salutation, as having eyes of a "flame of fire". This statement immediately recounts the passage of scripture in Matthew 3:11 where John the Baptist says He (Jesus) would baptize us with the Holy Ghost and with "fire". Jesus will bring the culmination of the already and not

---

[42] John Walvoord, The Revelation of Jesus Christ, (Chicago: Moody Press, 1966), WORDsearch CROSS e-book, 71-72.

yet Kingdom of God, and this verse is a foreshadow of what will happen later in the Revelation.

The words "burnished bronze," which describe His feet, translate a rare Greek word *chalkolibanō*, also used in 1:15. It seems to have been an alloy of several metals characterized by brilliance when polished.[43]

Christ's commendations of the church at Thyatira are extraordinary (2:19). The first commendation is for their works—their good deeds in Christ. He acknowledged their faith and love. These are spiritual virtues that are essential to Christian life and witness. They are the ground from which good works spring. These graces extended to ministerial functions in social, physical, and economic needs.

The second commendation is for their grace of patience. This word implies persistence in well doing even in the face of trials. The rest of this letter shows the trials of this church in its determination to live for Christ.

The third commendation, and the high point of this series of commendations, is that the good works and spiritual graces of the church at Thyatira increased amid oppression (2:19). The more these believers would attempt to remain pure the more intense their economic, social, and religious oppression would become. They could not join the trade guilds without compromising their holiness and testimony. Without this they were excluded from trade. Yet they increased in love, faith and works.[44]

Thyatira had the opposite problem that Ephesus had. Whereas, the Ephesian church had been good at dealing with

---

[43] John Walvoord and Roy Zuck, ed., The Bible Knowledge Commentary: An Exposition of the Scriptures by Dallas Seminary Faculty, (Colorado Springs, CO: Cook Communications, 1985), WORDsearch CROSS e-book, 937.

[44] R. Hollils Gause, Revelation: God's Stamp of Sovereignty on History, (Cleveland, TN: Pathway Press, 1998), WORDsearch CROSS e-book, 58.

false teachers but had lacked love, the church in Thyatira had lots of love but had become tolerant of false teachers. And, as was happening in Pergamum, the church in Thyatira was tolerating false teaching that was attempting to compromise with the pagan society.

In this case, the problem was Jezebel, who calls herself a prophet, a woman from among the believers, who claimed to have the gift of prophecy. She may indeed have had unusual gifts, but she was using her influence to teach positions that were contrary to God's word, misleading the believers. Like Balaam, she was leading the people into worship of idols and sexual sin (2:14-15), probably by teaching that immorality was not a serious matter for believers.

Her name may have been Jezebel, or John may have used the name Jezebel to symbolize the kind of evil she was promoting. Jezebel, a pagan Philistine queen of Israel, was considered the evilest woman who ever lived. She had led Israel's king, Ahab, into Baal worship and eventually had spread that idolatry throughout all of Israel (see 1 Kings 16:31-33; 19:1-2; 21:1-15; 2 Kings 9:7-10, 30-37).

"Jezebel" was being tolerated in the Thyatiran church. Perhaps her manner was so manipulative and persuasive that many did not notice, or perhaps no one realized the severe danger into which she was placing the entire church.

Most of the people in the city were tradesmen, so they belonged to various guilds. These guilds (such as potters, tentmakers, etc.) each had an area in the city and a guild hall, which functioned as a center for the guild's religious and civic activities. Usually the guild would hold a banquet at the hall once a week, and these banquets would often be centered on idolatry—featuring meat sacrificed to idols and, most likely, some form of sexual license as part of the revelry. Jezebel was probably encouraging the believers, mostly tradespeople themselves, to continue to take part in their guilds' activities as their civic duty. A refusal to join the guilds and take part in their activities would mean certain economic hardship. Jezebel suggested a way of compromise. Christ was pleased neither with this woman's teaching nor with the fact that the church tolerated her.[45]

Jesus' major condemnation concerned that woman Jezebel, who claimed to be a prophetess and taught believers to take part in the sexual immorality that accompanied pagan religion and to eat food sacrificed to idols. What was acceptable to that local society was abhorred by Christ. Their departure from morality had gone on for some time (v. 21). The church in Thyatira may have first heard the gospel from Lydia, converted through Paul's ministry (Acts 16:14-15). Interestingly now a woman, a self-claimed "prophetess," was influencing the church. Her name "Jezebel" suggests that she was corrupting the Thyatira church much like Ahab's wife Jezebel corrupted Israel (1 Kings 16:31-33). Christ promised sudden and immediate judgment, called her sin adultery, and promised that all who followed her would suffer intensely. He also promised, I will strike her children dead, meaning that suffering would extend also to her followers. The judgment would be so dramatic that all the churches would know that Christ is the One who searches hearts and minds.[46]

It is significant that having brought into judgment those who were evil in the church of Thyatira a special word is given to the godly remnant in this church. Here for the first time in the messages to the seven churches a group is singled out within a local church as being the continuing true testimony of the Lord. The godly remnant is described as not having or

---

[45] Barton B. Bruce et al., Life Application New Testament Commentary, (Wheaton, IL: Tyndale House, 2001), WORDsearch CROSS e-book, 1214.

[46] John Walvoord and Roy Zuck, ed., The Bible Knowledge Commentary: An Exposition of the Scriptures by Dallas Seminary Faculty, (Colorado Springs, CO: Cook Communications, 1985), WORDsearch CROSS e-book, Under: "3. Rebuke (2:20-23)".

holding the doctrine of Jezebel and as not knowing "the depths" or the deep things of Satan.

Here reference is made to the satanic system often seen in detail, in false cults which compete with the true Christian faith. Just as there are the deep things of God (1 Cor. 2:10), which are taught by the Spirit, so there are the deep things of Satan which result from his work.

The meaning of the expression "as they speak" is debatable. Alford believes that the subject of the verb "speak" is a reference to apostolic teaching embraced in the command which immediately follows: "I will put upon you none other burden." A parallel is found in Acts 15:28 where the council of Jerusalem determined, "It seemed good to the Holy Ghost, and to us, to lay upon you no greater burden than these necessary things." The clause is therefore an introduction to the material which follows rather than a conclusion of the material which preceded. As Alford summarizes it, "This act of simple obedience, and no deep matters beyond their reach, was what the Lord required of them."

To the godly remnant, then, Christ gives a limited responsibility. The evil character of the followers of Jezebel is such that they are beyond reclaim, but the true Christians are urged to hold fast to what they already have and await the coming of the Lord. It is remarkable that here first in the seven churches there is reference to the coming of Christ for His church as the hope of those who are engulfed by an apostate system.

As in the letters to the other churches, Christ closes His message to the church at Thyatira with a challenge to those who are overcomers. He promises that those who keep His works unto the end will be given a responsible position of judgment over the nations.

Closely following the prediction of a second coming, is this first reference in Revelation to the millennial reign of

Christ (cf., however, 1:6–7). The overcoming Christians are promised places of authority. They will share the rule of Christ over the nations of the world.

The word for "rule" (Gr., *poimanei*) means literally "to shepherd." Their rule will not be simply that of executing judgment, but also that of administering mercy and direction to those who are the sheep as contrasted to the goats (Matt. 25:31–46). The power to rule in this way was given to Christ by His heavenly Father (John 5:22).

To the overcomers also is given the promise of "the morning star." While various explanations of this expression have been given, it seems to refer to Christ Himself in His role as the returning One who will rapture the church before the dark hours preceding the dawn of the millennial kingdom.

The letter to the church at Thyatira closes with the familiar invitation to individuals who have ears to hear. Beginning with this letter this exhortation comes last in contrast to its position before the promise to overcomers in preceding letters. The word of Christ to the church of Thyatira is therefore addressed to any who will hear, who find themselves in similar need of this searching exhortation.[47]

Sardis

The city of Sardis was located about 30 miles southeast of Thyatira, on an important trade route that ran east and west through the kingdom of Lydia. Important industries included jewelry, dye, and textiles, which had made the city wealthy. From a religious standpoint it was a center of pagan worship and site of a temple of Artemis, which ruins remain as most of these cities in Asia are only in ruin. However, in the case of Sardis, a small village called Sart remains on the site of this

---

[47] John Walvoord, The Revelation of Jesus Christ, (Chicago: Moody Press, 1966), WORDsearch CROSS e-book, 77-78.

once-important city. Archeologists have discovered the ruins of a Christian church building next to the temple which many scholars hold to be this church.[48]

Jesus identifies Himself in verse 1 as the "the one who holds the "Seven Spirits of God, and the seven stars". This identification uses first the number seven which symbolizes completion or perfection in Scripture, particularly in the Book of Revelation (seven seals, seven trumpets, seven vials, seven years of tribulation, seven churches, etc.). Also, the Seven Spirits of God is linked to the seven-fold function of the Holy Spirit given in Isaiah 11:2-5. Then we see the seven stars, which are symbolic of the seven Pastors of the seven churches. This speaks of how God protects His anointed leaders.

The commendation is short and right to the point verse 1 where he says, "I know thy works". Some scholars even say the phrase "a name that thou livest" is also a commendation as they once were a church that was alive.

Since Jesus had the Spirit of God, this means that at one time the Spirit was active in this church. I like what J. Vernon McGee writes in His commentary: "My friend, the church today needs the Spirit of God working in it. We think we need methods, and we have all kinds of Band-Aid courses for believers in which you put on a little Band-Aid, and it will solve all your problems. What we really need to do is to get to the person of Christ whom only the Holy Spirit can make real and living to us. This is the thing Protestantism needs today."[49]

This brings us to their condemnation. It was that they had a name that they were alive, but they were dead! There is no

---

[48] John Walvoord and Roy Zuck, ed., The Bible Knowledge Commentary: An Exposition of the Scriptures by Dallas Seminary Faculty, (Colorado Springs, CO: Cook Communications, 1985), WORDsearch CROSS e-book, Under: "E. The Letter to the Church in Sardis (3:1-6)".

[49] J. Vernon McGee, Thru The Bible with J. Vernon McGee, (Nashville, TN: Thomas Nelson, 1983), WORDsearch CROSS e-book, Under: "CHAPTERS 2 AND 3".

indictment on a local church than one that is dead where people do not seem to care about their local parish to the extent that they let things go. Some let it go because of tradition (i.e. "We have always done it this way), or some may have let it die because of prejudice (i.e. "We do not want those type of people). Whatever the case here, they were known for a legacy, but failed to carry the legacy on. I agree with what one commentator writes: "Whenever a church stops preaching the gospel, it turns inward and self-destructs. When we get our eyes off the lost and focus on ourselves, we have lost our true spiritual vision. Churches that are not winning people to Christ are failing to obey the Great Commission (cf. Matt. 28:19-20). Without new converts, the church stagnates. When it stops growing, it starts to die."[50]

This was not an irretrievable situation, because there was still room for repentance and prospect for revival for this church. It is always Christ's will to give an opportunity for repentance and restoration, even if they have defected to the point of being called dead (2 Peter 3:9, 1 John 1:9) It is our attitude toward judgment which bars and discourages repentance, and does not reflect Christ's love and mercy toward us.

The rebuke of Christ continues with the phrase, "Become watchful, and establish the things that are about to die" (3:2). The verb tense implies that they had not been watchful and indeed they had not been doing what they were supposed to do. So, they must wake up to watchfulness and give attention these spiritual matters and activities in this church. The language suggests the idea that the point that death is imminent.

---

[50] Edward Hindson, Twenty-First Century Biblical Commentary Series – The Book of Revelation: Unlocking the Future, ed. Mal Couch and Ed Hindson, (Chattanooga, TN: AMG Publishers, 2002), WORDsearch CROSS e-book, 44.

Christ's criticism of the works of the people of Sardis is that their works had not accomplished what God had in mind to do when He gave the gifts: "For your works I have not found fulfilled before my God" (3:2). There are two spiritual principles here. The first is the principle of the waste of their spirituality. A gift or ministry which is being neglected is in process of becoming extinct. The second principle is righteous judgment. A spiritual gift is given in stewardship. It will be withdrawn from a church that does not exercise its stewardship.

The rebuke is followed by a saving exhortation: "Remember therefore how thou has received and heard, and hold fast, and repent" (3:3). They are called to remember the message that had saved them from sin, and to continue in the work of God (Ephesians 2:8-10). This is the heart of repentance. There is no point in wallowing in nostalgia for past joys, revivals, and glory. This is not repentance, it is remembrance.

The letter now turns to the consequences to be faced if they do not heed this warning: "Unless you are watchful, I will come to you as a thief, and you will not know in what hour I come to you" (3:3). The city of Sardis was often raided by robber bands which surrounded them. Their presumption as a city left them vulnerable to these attacks. In the church their slumber left them open to Christ's coming as a thief. He would take from them the treasures in which they took presumptuous and nostalgic pride. They were so dull spiritually that they would not even know that the "thief" had come.

There were those in Sardis who were to be commended: "But you have a few names in Sardis which have not soiled their garments" (3:4). This commendation is not to the whole church but to a scarce and pure remnant.

There is a promise to overcomers attached to the commendation: "And they will walk with me in white because they are worthy" (3:4). This is the promise of eternal life. The white garments stand in contrast to the soiled garments of their neighbors. The white garments given in the Day of Judgment correspond to the way they have kept their garments pure in age. To be clothed in white is a frequently used symbol of reward in the age to come (4:4; 6:11; 7:9, 13).

In verse four the promise had been specifically to those in Sardis who had not defiled their garments. In verse five Christ makes a promise to all those who will overcome. It is a promise beyond Sardis to any church and to any believer in any age. This basic promise is expanded into three promises.

The first of these is that the overcomer will be clothed in white garments. This is an expansion and a more specific application of the promise, in verse four. The passive voice verb is frequently used to ascribe an action to God. So, this promise is that God will clothe the overcomer in white garments. The awarding of these garments of righteousness is an event of judgment in the age to come.

The second promise is, "And I will not at all [double negative] wipe out his name out of the book of life" (3:5). The promise of life is unequivocal; it is personally extended by Christ. He is both Lord and Judge and He has the authority over the book of life. The names written there are by His authority, and the blotting out of a name is under His authority.

The book of life is the record of the redeemed. The idea of such a book appears in the Old Testament (Exodus 32:32, 33; Psalm 69:28; Daniel 12:1). The specific phrase "book of life" is used in the New Testament to represent the redemption of those whose names are in it. To have one's name written in the book of life is to be protected in this life (Revelation 13:8; 17:8). The book of life is determinative for salvation or damnation at the throne of God's judgment (20:12, 15). To have one's name written in the book of life is essential to entering the holy city (21:27).

The third promise is, "And I will confess his name before my Father and before his angels" (3:5). Christ's confession of a believer's name in the day of judgment will be based on the presence of that name in the book of life. The act of confession on Christ's part is an act of judgment (Mark 8:38). It is also an act of redemption because the Redeemer and the redeemed are one (Hebrews 2:11-13).

This is a judgment scene. The confession is made in the presence of the Father and His angels. Christ often represented His coming in glory and in judgment in these terms (Matthew 16:27; Mark 8:38; Matthew 26:64; Luke 9:26).[51]

Philadelphia

The message to the church at Philadelphia is in some respects one of the most fascinating of all the messages to the churches. Here is a church which was faithful to Christ and the Word of God.

The city of Philadelphia itself, known in modern times as Alasehir, is in Lydia some twenty-eight miles southeast of Sardis and was named after a king of Pergamos, Attalus Philadelphus, who built the city. The word Philadelphia, meaning "brotherly love," is found six other times in the New Testament (Rom. 12:10; 1 Thess. 4:9; Heb. 13:1; 1 Peter 1:22; 2 Peter 1:7). Here the word occurs for the seventh and final time, but only here is it used of the city bearing this name.

The city of Philadelphia had an extended history and several times was almost destroyed by earthquakes. The most recent rebuilding was in 17 AD. The land area around Philadelphia was rich in agricultural value but had noticeable tokens of previous volcanic action.

---

[51] R. Hollils Gause, Revelation: God's Stamp of Sovereignty on History, (Cleveland, TN: Pathway Press, 1998), WORDsearch CROSS e-book, 63-66.

Grapes were one of the principal crops, and, in keeping with this, Dionysus was one of the chief objects of pagan worship. Through the spans, a nominal Christian testimony continued in this city of Philadelphia and prospered even under Turkish rule. But all nominal Christians left the city for Greece after World War I.

The message addressed to the church at Philadelphia has the rare characteristic of being almost entirely a word of praise, like that received by the church at Smyrna, but in sharp difference to the messages to Sardis and Laodicea.[52]

Philadelphia was a small church in a difficult area with no prestige and no wealth, discouraged because it had not grown. But Christ had no words of rebuke for this small, seemingly insignificant church, and he described himself to the church in Philadelphia as the one who is holy and true. This title was a familiar title for God (see Isaiah 40:25; Habakkuk 3:3; Mark 1:24; John 6:69).

For Christ to hold the key of David means that he has the authority to open the door to his future Kingdom. This alludes to an event recorded in Isaiah 22:15-25, when the official position of secretary of state in Judah was taken from Shebna and given to Eliakim. God through Isaiah said to Eliakim: "I will give him the key to the house of David—the highest position in the royal court. He will open doors, and no one will be able to shut them; he will close doors, and no one will be able to open them" (Isaiah 22:22).

Christ holds absolute power and authority over entrance into his future Kingdom. After the door is opened, no one can shut it—salvation is assured. Once it is shut, no one can open it—judgment is certain.[53]

---

[52] John Walvoord, The Revelation of Jesus Christ, (Chicago: Moody Press, 1966), WORDsearch CROSS e-book, 83-84.

[53] Barton B. Bruce et al., Life Application New Testament Commentary, (Wheaton, IL: Tyndale House, 2001), WORDsearch CROSS e-book, 1217.

In verse 7, the phrases "who opens, and no one will shut," and "who shuts and no one opens" refer to the divine sovereignty of Jesus Christ.

Just as Eliakim had free access to King Hezekiah's palace, so Christ has free access to the heavenly palace. He alone can take us into the Father's house. Jesus said, "I am the way, and the truth, and the life: no one comes to the Father, but through Me" (John 14:6). Thus, it is that access to the heavenly palace is through Jesus Christ and no other.

In a similar analogy, our Lord said, "Enter by the narrow gate; for the gate is wide, and the way is broad that leads to destruction, and many are those who enter by it. For the gate is small, and the way is narrow, that leads to life, and few are those who find it" (Matt. 7:13-14).

But thank God, Jesus came to give us the "keys of the kingdom" (Matt. 16:19), that we might use them to open the door of heaven, to all who would enter, by faith in Jesus Christ.[54]

There really is no condemnation to this church except the brief phrase "thou hast a little strength." To me the author, this shows the need for revival to even the strongest church.

The church in Philadelphia received no rebuke from Christ. Instead they were commended and given a promise because they had been willing to endure patiently. The promise was, I will also keep you from the hour of trial that is going to come upon the whole world to test those who live on the earth. This is an explicit promise that the Philadelphia church will not endure the hour of trial, which is unfolded, beginning in Revelation 6. Christ was saying that the Philadelphia church would not enter the future time of trouble;

---

[54] Edward Hindson, Twenty-First Century Biblical Commentary Series – The Book of Revelation: Unlocking the Future, ed. Mal Couch and Ed Hindson, (Chattanooga, TN: AMG Publishers, 2002), WORDsearch CROSS e-book, 46.

He could not have stated it more explicitly. If Christ had meant to say that they would be preserved through a time of trouble, or would be taken out from within the Tribulation, a different verb and a different preposition would have been required. Though scholars have attempted to avoid this conclusion in order to affirm post-tribulationism, the combination of the verb "keep" (tērein) with the preposition "from" (ek) is in sharp contrast to the meaning of keeping the church "through" (dia), a preposition which is not used here. The expression "the hour of trial" (a time period) makes it clear that they would be kept out of that period. It is difficult to see how Christ could have made this promise to this local church if it were God's intention for the entire church to go through the Tribulation that will come on the entire world. Even though the church at Philadelphia would go to glory via death long before the time of trouble would come, if the church here is taken to be typical of the body of Christ standing true to the faith, the promise seems to go beyond the Philadelphia church, to all those who are believers in Christ.[55]

The promises to overcomers are four-fold after the announcement of verse 10:

- Pillar in the temple of God. Just as massive pillars supported ancient temples, so the believers will be secure in their position in God's heavenly temple.
- Name of God. God's name reflects His character. Having His name written on us symbolizes having His character indelibly inscribed on our hearts and lives.
- Name of city of God. The promise of the New Jerusalem reminds us that we are destined for the heavenly city where the Church will reign triumphant.

---

[55] John Walvoord and Roy Zuck, ed., The Bible Knowledge Commentary: An Exposition of the Scriptures by Dallas Seminary Faculty, (Colorado Springs, CO: Cook Communications, 1985), WORDsearch CROSS e-book, 939.

Our "right of citizenship" has already been guaranteed.

- Christ's new name. His "new name" indicates the full revelation of His character. The Scripture promises, "We know that, when He appears, we shall be like Him, because we shall see Him just as He is" (1 John 3:2). [56]

Laodicea

Laodicea was probably one of the most well-known of the cities in Asia Minor. The city was in the southwest of Phrygia, on the river Lycus, not far from Colosse, and lying between it and Philadelphia.

It was destroyed by an earthquake, A.D. 62. It was then rebuilt by its wealthy citizens without the help of the state [Tacitus, Annals, 14.27]. This wealth (arising from the excellence of its wools) led to a self-satisfied, lukewarm state, concerning spiritual things, as described in Revelation 3:17.

Paul's Epistle to the Colossians is thought to have been written to the Laodicean Church. Paul specifically mentions this church, in Colossians 4:16. The Church, in latter times, was apparently flourishing; for one of the councils at which the canon of Scripture was determined was held in Laodicea in A.D. 361. There is a Christian hardly that can be found there today. [57]

Christ, in the salutation, introduces Himself as "the Amen" in addressing the angel of the church "in" Laodicea, as

---

[56] Edward Hindson, Twenty-First Century Biblical Commentary Series – The Book of Revelation: Unlocking the Future, ed. Mal Couch and Ed Hindson, (Chattanooga, TN: AMG Publishers, 2002), WORDsearch CROSS e-book, 47.

[57] Robert Jamieson, A.R. Fausset, David Brown, A Commentary: Critical, Experimental, and Practical on the Old and New Testaments, (Toledo, OH: Jerome B. Names & Co., 1884), WORDsearch CROSS e-book, Under: "Chapter 3".

the best texts read, instead of "the church of the Laodiceans." The frequent use of Amen, meaning "so be it," is a feature of the declarations of Christ and is usually translated "verily," or used as an ending to a prayer. As a title of Christ, this term indicates His dominion and the inevitability of the fulfillment of His promises. When Christ speaks, it is the final word, and His will is always affected and fulfilled either immediately or gradually.

Christ is called the Faithful and true Witness in contrast to the church in Laodicea which was neither faithful nor true. Christ had been earlier introduced as "the faithful witness" in 1:5 and as "he that is true" in 3:7. The fact that Christ is both a faithful and a true witness gives special solemnity to the words which follow, and confirms the Canonical context of Revelation.

Finally, He is described as "the beginning of the creation of God." As "the beginning" (Gr., arche), He is not the first of creation, but He is before all creation.[58] This would make the reader think of the Gospel of John where He is described as being at the beginning in John 1:1-4.

There is really no commendation for this church because as Christ expounds on this church's works, they are neither hot nor cold but lukewarm. The word cold here would seem to denote the state where there was no pretension to religion, where everything was utterly lifeless and dead. The language is obviously figurative, but it is such as is often employed, when we speak of one as being cold towards another, as having a cold or icy heart, etc. The word hot would denote, of course, the opposite—warm and zealous in their love and service. The very words that we are constrained to use when speaking on this subject-such words as ardent, (i.e. hot, or burning;) fervid, (i.e. very hot, burning, boiling)-show how necessary it is to use

---

[58] John Walvoord, The Revelation of Jesus Christ, (Chicago: Moody Press, 1966), WORDsearch CROSS e-book, 90.

such words, and how common it is. The state indicated here, therefore, would be that in which there was a profession of religion, but no warm-hearted piety; in which there was not, on the one hand, open and honest opposition to him, and, on the other, such warm-hearted and honest love as he had a right to look for among his professed friends; in which there was a profession of that religion which ought to warm the heart with love, and fill the soul with zeal in the cause of the Redeemer; but where the only result, in fact, was deadness and indifference to him and his cause. Among those who made no profession, he had reason to expect nothing but coldness; among those who made a profession, he had a right to expect the glow of a warm affection, but he found nothing but indifference.[59]

Lukewarmness is indecisive and indistinct. It neither refreshes nor heals. It is contrary to the character of Christ and to those who have a vital relationship with Him. The Laodicean lukewarmness offered no confrontation of the world and no distinctive witness of Jesus. It is insipid and nauseating; so, Christ gives this judgment: "Because you are neither cold nor hot, I am about to vomit you out of my mouth" (3:16). In other words, it made God sick on how this church went from serving Him, to outside of it later in the story.

The spiritual condition at Laodicea was also a proud and prideful condition. The presumptuous and lethargic lifestyle of the city had corrupted the church. They boasted of their wealth: "I am rich, and I have become (and still am) increased with goods, and I need nothing" (3:17; Luke 12:19). The people of this church had received of the wealth of the city. They were not persecuted nor were they excluded from the trade of the city. They had no sense of needing anything from God, that they had not already supplied for themselves. They

---

[59] Albert Barnes, Barnes' Notes on the New Testament, ed. Robert Frew, WORDsearch CROSS e-book, Under: "Revelation of John 3".

interpreted their possessions and position as indications of their spirituality (1 Timothy 6:5; Luke 12:15).

Christ's assessment was the opposite in all respects. These people were ignorant; they did not even know their spiritual condition (Revelation 3:17). Everything they boasted of, they needed.

Each of the terms used here to describe Laodicea is a symbol of spiritual need. Instead of being noble, they were wretched (cf. Romans 7:24 where the same word is used). They were miserable (cf. 1 Corinthians 15:19 where the same word is used). Poverty is a frequently used symbol of spiritual need; these people were characterized as beggars. It is not simply that they had no surplus; they had nothing at all. Blindness represents spiritual darkness; it is also associated with being a beggar in the society to which this letter is addressed. This description suggests the picture of the blind beggars who lined the streets of the cities of that day. Nakedness is a symbol of shame; people were humiliated as punishment by having their clothes stripped from them, or by being shorn to the buttocks. In a city of wealth and expensive clothing these people were humiliated with their spiritual nakedness.

The Laodiceans felt the need of no one's help. They thought themselves to be wealthy beyond need or threat of poverty, but they were beggars—blind beggars in the city famous for their healing of the blind with their famous eyesalve. In the city famous for its fine wool, they were naked. This reminds one of the modern churches of today. The false doctrines of today such as the Word of Faith Movement, the Social Gospel, and other doctrines are putting the church in a Laodicean State.

This is the most severe condemnation contained in all the seven letters. Yet, it is followed by the most endearing invitation to repentance contained in the letters. The condition of Laodicea was severe, but it was not beyond the grace of God (Romans 5:20).

Christ's counsel is promised: "I counsel you to buy of me." (Revelation 3:18). Christ offers them gold, garments, and eye salve.

The gold that Christ offers is pure gold—purified by fire. Gold is a symbol of spiritual wealth; in this case it has been made as pure as it can be. To the idea of wealth Christ adds the idea of purity. The impurities have been removed from the gold by being "boiled out." This symbolism was foreign to the thinking of this church. They did not know the nature of persecution and trial.

The garments that Christ offers are special. Their proud symbol of wealthy apparel was the fine black wool of Laodicea. Instead Christ offers them white garments—the garments of holiness and victory. It is the clothing of the saints in heaven (3:5; 6:11) and of the twenty-four elders (4:4). These garments would cover the shame of their backslidings. Christ urged these people to buy eyesalve from Him to rub on their eyes in order that they might see. Their blindness was spiritual, and they needed the Balm of Gilead (Jeremiah 46:11, 12). They lived in a city famous for its eyesalve, but still they were blind.

There are common factors in all of these offers from Christ. He is the Giver of gold purified in fire. He is the Supplier of the white garments and the Fuller who makes them white. He is the healing Balm in the eyesalve.

By His rebuke and the corrections promised, Christ assures the Laodiceans of His love: "Whomever I love I rebuke, and I chastise" (Revelation 3:19; Proverbs 3:11, 12). In this quotation Christ is the Speaker; He is, God who speaks the promise. Christ uses the word *phileo* for love. It carries the concepts of *agapao*, but it also carries the intimacy of friendship (John 15:13, 14). It is in this love that He exposes and rebukes sin. The word "chastise" certainly includes punishment, but it is broader. It carries the idea of a total program of child training. This is a relationship of love and friendship. He does not threaten them but reassures them. The aim of Christ's rebuke is restoration. So, the exhortation follows: "Be zealous and repent" (Revelation 3:19).

Our Lord closes the letter to the Laodiceans with two conditional promises. The first is the promise that He will enter a place of fellowship with anyone who hears His knocking and who opens the door. He describes Himself: "Behold I stand at the door, and I am knocking" (3:20). He has been excluded from the church; He is outside knocking and asking to be admitted. "In an act of unbelievable condescension, he requests permission to enter and re-establish fellowship." This is an announcement of His love and patience. Christ had promised that His Father would open the door to anyone who knocked (Luke 11:9, 10). Now the question is, "Will the church open to Him when He knocks?" This is a question for the individual as well as the church.

There are two promises given here. The first is that Christ will enter and establish fellowship. Eating with His disciples represents Christ's fellowship with them in the Lord's supper and in the Marriage Supper of the Lamb; it also means the fulfillment of the kingdom of God (Luke 22:15-18; Rev. 19:9).

The second promise is that of sitting with Christ in His throne (3:21). This is the victory of the one who endures until the end. It is a promise to be fulfilled in the last day—at the time of judgment. Christ will share His exaltation and authority with those who overcome in Him. Christ is our King; by His redeeming act He makes us kings. This inheritance is parallel with Christ's own inheritance from the Father (cf. Romans 8:17, 18). The only begotten Son was obedient to His heavenly Father and He was victorious. The Father rewarded Him by raising Him up and exalting Him over all things (Philippians 2:5-11; Ephesians 1:20-23). The Father shared His throne with the Son (Hebrews 1:3). This is the pattern of our inheritance with Christ. What His Father did for Him, the Son promises to do for those who overcome in Him.[60]

[60] R. Hollils Gause, Revelation: God's Stamp of Sovereignty on History, (Cleveland, TN: Pathway Press, 1998), WORDsearch CROSS e-book, 74-77.

3

IN THE SPIRIT
IN HEAVEN:
REVELATION 4-16

(**Author's Note*: You will notice that much of the remainder of this commentary is offered in more of an outline form. This will allow the text to be more concise and understandable to the reader.)

Revelation Chapter 4

As Revelation 4 opens, John sees an open door in heaven. This reminds readers of the opened door that Jesus placed to the church at Philadelphia (3:8).

The verb in the Greek which is passive in form shows a divine passive indicating that the door was opened by God. The perfect tense of this verb suggests that the door had been opened and continues to be opened for John and others.[61]

Revelation 4:2 - *The Throne*

The throne is revealed in the center of heaven. This points to the centrality of God. God must be at the center of our universe.[62]

Revelation 4:3 - *The Rainbow*

The throne is encircled by a rainbow. This is a reminder of The Noahic Covenant, which God made with Noah in Genesis after the flood (Genesis 9:13).

The Rainbow, and the things that accompany it, would also make one think of the previous visions of Ezekiel (1:26).

Revelation 4:4 - *The 24 Elders*

These Elders are also mentioned in 5:6-14, 7:11-13, 11:16, 14:3, and 19:4.

There are a number of schools of thought on the 24 Elders, including:

- 12 Tribes of Israel and 12 Apostles of the Lamb.
- Heavenly Angelic Counselors.
- Representatives of the Raptured Church.

Most scholars hold the position supporting the first school of thought over the other two.

Elders were leaders who represented the people of God or community of the Church (In Exodus, Moses, and in Acts, the

---

[61] John Christopher Thomas, Two Horizons Commentary: Revelation, (Grand Rapids, Michigan: Wm. B. Eerdmans Publishing Company, 2016), 226

[62] Craig R. Koester: Revelation and the End of All Things, Grand Rapids, Eerdmans, 2001, 73

Church). The twelve Tribes of Israel and the twelve Apostles have a significant place in Heaven (7:4-8) and the New Jerusalem (21:12-14).

The Identity is also confirmed by the description of the white garments and golden crowns. This fulfills the eschatological promise of Jesus in 3:5.[63]

Revelation 4:5 - *The Seven Lamps burning before the fire, which are the seven Spirits of God*

In the Greek, attention is given that these are torches. Usually, in the Scripture, a torch would allude to the judgment of God. When one thinks of the Seven Spirits of God, they are immediately drawn to the Old Testament passage, of Isaiah 11:2.

The term fire makes one also think of the passages about the Holy Spirit in Matthew 3:11, which speaks of being baptized "with the Holy Ghost and with Fire."

Huros is the Greek term used in both Revelation 4.5 and Matthew 3.11[64]

This author feels that the fire in Matt 3.11 speaks of judgment. The Holy Spirit is a last day sign, as stated in Acts, chapter 2. As the Holy Spirit is the "blessing" in the last day, the "fire" is the judgment side of the Holy Spirit, working in trinitarian family with the wrath of God and the wrath of the Lamb terminology.

Revelation 4:6-9 - *The Four Living Creatures*

The four living creatures are around the throne. This shows how life revolves around God.

---

[63] Thomas, 226.

[64] Robby Waddell, The Spirit of the Book of Revelation, Blandford Forum, Deo Publishing, 2006, 17

They are living creatures- alive by the decree of God. They are attendants around the throne and servants to the One on the throne.

This is reminiscent of scenes in Ezekiel 1 and Isaiah 6.

The Creatures Appearance:

- A Lion
- A Calf
- A Face as of a Man
- An Eagle

Their function is to offer a continual praise to God.

Revelation 4:10-11 - Worship Scene

They are worshipping God as the Creator. No doubt, they are referring to the God of the Old Testament.

Now, we find a transition. Beginning in Chapter 5, He is worshipped as the God of the New Testament.

Revelation Chapter 5

Revelation 5:1 - And I Saw

When this literary marker is used in the Book of Revelation, it means the start of something new to the vision.

There are several notable observations in this verse:

- The Scroll being in the right hand of the One who sits on it continues to place emphasis on the authority of Jesus.
- The fact that the scroll is on the right hand symbolizes its importance.
- This scroll reminds the reader of the one that is in Ezekiel because it has writing both on the inside and the outside.[65]

---

[65] R. Hollis Gause, Revelation: God's Stamp of Sovreignty on History, Cleveland, Pathway Press, 1998, 91

Sealed with seven seals

- Seals upon legal documentation were placed there by witnesses.
- This indicates the trustworthiness and authenticity of the document.

There are many schools of thought to what this seven-sealed book represents.

Some say this represents the Lamb's book of life. This does not seem to be feasible, due to the fact the book is already written and sealed.

Others say this represents the Old Testament, revealed in the New Testament. However, this position does not seem legitimate because the Old Testament prophecies were not concealed.

Roman law required a seal to be sealed seven times. True, but we are not dealing with Roman law.

A few declare this to be Daniel's Prophecy revealed in John's Day- A partial truth but not the sealed book.

These seals represents events recorded in Revelation. This is the title deed of earth's redemption- Zech 14:9.[66]

Revelation 5:2-4 - *Who is worthy to open the seals?*

The angel conducts a search, here, that turns up nothing. No one was able to open the seal. John weeps because no one was able to open the seal.[67]

The word weep, here, is used very strongly in the Greek, to depict deep mourning and violent weeping. It is used here in the imperfect tense, to suggest that John kept on weeping as

---

[66] Voorhis, 17-19

[67] Voorhis, 17-19

though he could not be consoled. The same context can be seen in Revelation 6:10 when the question is asked, "how long oh Lord?"

Revelation 5:5-7 - Weep Not

The Elder identifies the one who has overcome, as the Lion of the Tribe of Judah and the Root of David.

Lion of the Tribe of Judah relates to the Patriarchal blessing spoken by Joseph to Judah in Genesis 49:8-12.

The Root of David would make the reader think back to chapter 3:7 with the key of David.

Then, Jesus is identified as the Lamb that was slain. This gives several meanings to the hearers:

- The Passover lamb of the exodus story
- The Fourth Gospel- John 1:29
- The Lamb is alive hear giving premise that He is no longer dead (1:18, 2:8)

The seven horns speak of complete power.

Having taken the book gives a complete victory in Jesus.

Revelation 5:8-14- Another Worship Scene

The "prayers of the Saints" reference shows the urgency of the people of God praying in the last day.

The mention of singing a new song reminds us that we are to praise God. The song shows qualifications of worthiness:

- Slaughtered
- Purchased
- He has Made

A shift is made by the elders and the creatures, from being outside to around the throne. Worship must press us into the presence of God.[68]

Revelation 6-8:1

Revelation 6:1-2

The most prominent theories concerning the identity of the white horse rider are as follows:

o The white horse rider represents Christ and the beginning of tribulation.
o The white horse rider represents the righteous judgments of God.
o The white horse rider represents the going forth of the Gospel of Christ to conquer in the end time.
o The white horse rider represents the Anti-Christ and his coming forth to establish his kingdom.

In the interpretation of these verses we need to understand that this horse rider is NOT Christ, in that we have had him come to rapture the Church in Revelation 4:1, and that He comes back riding on a white horse in Revelation 19. Plus, if you note the rider's description, he is representative of war, to conquer, in the very next seals that are loosed.

Revelation 6:2 "And I saw and behold a white horse: and he that sat on him <u>had a bow; and a crown was given unto him: and he went forth conquering, and to conquer."</u>

He wears a crown, though it is the (stephanos) crown of paste and glass, and the weathering laurel wreath rather than the true (diadema) of rulership. He has a weapon, but it is a bow, not a sword (which represents the Word of God).

The fact that war, famine, and death follow this rider is

---

[68] Thomas, 260-267

also a key to his identity. The Anti-Christ will fight no less than 5 major wars in 7 years. This, as well as the judgments of God, will cause famine and death. The fact of the many martyrs referred to suggests the Anti-Christ is actively persecuting the saints of God early in his reign.[69]

Revelation 6:3

This is the opening of the second seal, which represents war. The Antichrist will not only come to power with war, but will also come into power during war. In fact, as we read in Ezekiel 38-39, there will be a war going on to bring him into prominence, and to make a seven-year treaty with Israel which he will break in the middle of the tribulation.

Revelation 6:4-5

Famine is now the third seal. The black horse rider had a pair of balances in his hand for the purpose of measuring food. This is a symbol of famine. Bread by measure and weight signifies scarcity of food (Ezek. 4:10-17). The penny referred to be a day's wage (Mt. 20:1-16), and a measure (nearly a quart) of corn was a slave's daily ration, an amount usually purchasable for one-eighth of a penny.

Revelation 6:6-8

Death is the fourth seal. The color of the horse is pale—literally a pale yellowish green—the color of putridness and corruption (6:8). This is an appropriate color for death and the grave.

There are two unique aspects of this seal. First, the rider of the horse is named. His name is Death. The name represents his character and his power.

---

[69] Voorhis, 179

Second, this rider is accompanied by another. He also is named. His name is Hades (6:8). His name also represents his character and power. The name Hades refers to the entire region of the dead with its corruption and decay.

This double imagery intensifies the picture. Death is followed by Hades. In the wake of the rider of the horse is decay. These two are given specific authority. They do not possess this authority in themselves. As with the other horses and riders, the authority is from the Lamb. The specific authority which these riders have is over a fourth part of the earth (6:8). The one-fourth represents a population segment and not a geographical segment. This figure shows that this plague will be vast, but it will not afflict everyone, except indirectly. There will be misery and ease in the world at the same time.

The authority given to these two is to kill. The instruments of this pestilence are the sword, hunger, death, and wild beasts. God called them "My four sore judgments" (Ezekiel 14:21).

The sword (romphaia) is the large two-edged sword used in war and persecution. Hunger is the culmination and intensification of the famine of the black horse and its rider.

Death is at the epidemic level. It is a pestilence. This is an intensification of all the preceding judgments. Wild beasts become a threat to human life in times such as are here described. Old Testament prophecies had predicted similar acts of judgment (Jeremiah 15:3; Ezekiel 5:17).[70]

Revelation 6:9-11

If the rapture has already occurred at this point (and this author believes it will have), these martyrs must be those slain

---

[70] R. Hollils Gause, Revelation: God's Stamp of Sovereignty on History, (Cleveland, TN: Pathway Press, 1998), WORDsearch CROSS e-book, 106.

by the Anti-Christ and false religious system which help bring him to power.

Revelation 6:12-17

The sixth seal transitions the scene back to the physical world. The first five judgments had been directed toward specific areas, but this judgment was over the whole world. The entire population would be afraid when the earth itself trembled.

With the opening of the sixth seal, there was a great earthquake, which is followed by other cosmic disturbances. To properly understand these events, we must go beyond the literal meaning.

These word pictures were common to many of John's readers and stood for the coming "day of the Lord" or "day of judgment."

o The earthquake in Scripture always pictures God's presence (see Exodus 19:18; Isaiah 2:19-21; Haggai 2:6).
o The color of the sun is that of cloth worn in times of mourning.
o The moon will appear red due to whatever in the atmosphere caused the sun to be darkened.
o The stars falling to earth could refer to a terrifying meteor shower with meteors striking the earth (see Mark 13:21-25).
o The disappearance of mountains and islands will probably result from the great earthquake (see Hebrews 12:26-27).
o Finally, the sky will roll up like a scroll (see also Isaiah 34:4).

Those who would interpret this book as chronological will consider this to be the end of the first round of judgments.

Those who picture the book as cyclical, or as showing varying intensity with all the judgments ending at the return of Christ, see the rolling up of the sky as the time when Christ opens heaven and returns to earth (19:11).[71]

The contents of Revelation, chapter 6, should put to rest the false teachings that God--being a God of love--could not judge a wicked world. It also raises the important question contained in the closing words of verse 17: Who can stand? Only those who have availed themselves of the grace of God before the time of judgment will be able to stand when God deals with the earth in this final period of great distress.[72]

Revelation 7

Revelation chapter seven deals with two groups of people. First, it deals with the 144,000 Jews. Second, it deals with the tribulation saints. Let us look at this in more detail.

Revelation 7:1-8

Note the Following Observations:

- In Revelation Chapter 6 we see God's interpretation and direction in world history which is judgment.
- In Revelation Chapter 7 we see God's plan for salvation history.
- God promised to save Israel
- God's plan to save mankind of all nations

Notice in the first part of this passage that the angel is from the rising of the sun, showing his close proximity to God,

---

[71] Barton B. Bruce et al., Life Application New Testament Commentary, (Wheaton, IL: Tyndale House, 2001), WORDsearch CROSS e-book, 1225-1226.

[72] John Walvoord and Roy Zuck, ed., The Bible Knowledge Commentary: An Exposition of the Scriptures by Dallas Seminary Faculty, (Colorado Springs, CO: Cook Communications, 1985), WORDsearch CROSS e-book, 949.

and that he has the seal of the "living" God which shows the authority of God over death.

We see the souls under the altar, in chapter 6, and now the living God! First, He seals the 144,000. It is interesting to note that these represent the 12 tribes of Israel. Then, we see in verses 9 and following in Chapter 7, the great multitude of every nation, tribe, and tongue.

The Mid-Tribulationist holds that this is the rapture of the church, while the Pre-Tribulationist holds that this is the complete fulfillment of the promises. Whichever view one takes on the rapture here, whether it be Pre, Mid, or Post, the following things are evident:

- This is God's fulfillment to the Patriarchs of the Old Testament.
- Paul spoke of this in Romans 11:5, 12, 15, 26
- Since these numbers are symbolic, they are numbers of a perfected remnant, a remnant that stands for God's completion of the Abraham Covenant.

Other religions hold various views. For instance, the Jehovah's Witnesses believe this to be adherents to their faith. When they celebrate communion, only the one of the 144,000 can partake of it.

Revelation 7:9-17

This allows the same community (Christ's) from two different perspectives. In verses 1-8, we see Israel, but in verses 9-17 we see many tribes, nations, tongues, and peoples.

The Lamb conquers through his death, and this is celebrated by his followers by waving palm branches. In both the Bible and the Apocrypha, this is a symbol of victory (7:9, and in 1 Macc. 13:51).

What is amazing to me is the element of the already and not yet kingdom of God, being brought out here with the palm branches waved in the gospels before the Lamb's slaughter, and now here, with the conquering authority and power of the Lamb. The palm branches are once again waved, to symbolize the victory during tribulation.

There is then another worship scene, which ushers in the seventh seal. This begins the sounding of the seven trumpets. We also see hear a prophetic utterance of what is to come in verses 16-17, which is fulfilled in Revelation 21.

Revelation 8

Revelation 8:1-5

The opening of the seventh seal is quite complex, because the following are covered:

o silence in heaven for a half an hour.
o seven angels preparing the seven trumpet judgments.
o the golden altar with the prayers of the saints denoting worship.
o thundering, lightnings, and earthquakes.

Chris Thomas points out, in his commentary on Revelation, that the silence in heaven impacted John and the hearers of that day of prophecy in several ways. First, there is an expectation of a final activity of God, but instead there is silence. Second, it reminds the readers of past moments of silence in the prophetic call of God (Habakkuk 2:20, Zechariah 2:13, Zephaniah 1:7,). Third, it could produce a time of reflection of the mercy of God during the wrath of God.[73]

Robby Waddell, in his book the Spirit of the Book of Revelation, notes that the seven trumpets are the contents of the seventh seal. The description of the trumpet blasts increases in length as the judgments now begin to intensify much like the progression of the seals. [74]

---

[73] Thomas, 315
[74] Waddell, 141

The Golden altar and prayer still give a sense of intercession even in chaotic times. This is a common theme throughout, not just the Apocalypse, but the Word of God as well.

The thundering, lightning, and earthquakes once again place an emphasis on total judgment with the seven trumpets getting ready to sound on the inhabitants of the earth. Now, the natural elements once again are jolted.

Revelation 8:7- The First Trumpet- Vegetation struck

The readers of the time that Revelation was written would have immediately thought of the plagues God sent upon Egypt in the book of Exodus.

The first reference of hail is accompanied by two other references in the Apocalypse (Revelation 11:19 and 16:21).

The reference of fire can immediately make one think of the previous references of fire, such as fire from the altar, wrath of fire, and with the fact that it is mixed with blood symbolize the souls under the altar as far as relating to the blood being on their hands during the wrath of the Lamb.

Revelation 8:8-9- The Second Trumpet- The Seas Struck

Revelation 8:8-9 "And the second angel sounded, and as it were a great mountain burning with fire was cast into the sea: and the third part of the sea became blood; And the third part of the creatures which were in the sea, and had life, died; and the third part of the ships were destroyed."

- 1/3 of the ships
- 1/3 of the fish
- 1/3 of the sea filled with blood

In 1982, the world's merchant fleet totaled 45,000 ships. During this period, the US spent $20 billion for new ships for the navy. Given the world's vessels then totaling 48,000, had this taken place during that time 16,000 ships would have been destroyed. It is also estimated that had this taken place during that time, over a half-million people would have lost their life.

Revelation 8:9-10

The Third Trumpet- The Waters Struck

Revelation 8:10-11 "And the third angel sounded, and there fell a great star from heaven, burning as it were a lamp, and it fell upon the third part of the rivers, and upon the fountains of waters; And the name of the star is called Wormwood: and the third part of the waters became wormwood; and many men died of the waters, because they were made bitter.

This trumpet attacks our water supply and poisons the water.

The word bitterness here in the Greek and Wormwood in the Greek both mean calamities. This speaks of water being made into poison by this.[75]

Revelation 8:12-13- The Fourth Trumpet- The Heaven's Struck

Revelation 8:12-13 And the fourth angel sounded, and the third part of the sun was smitten, and the third part of the

---

[75] Voorhis, 45

moon, and the third part of the stars; so as the third part of them was darkened, and the day shone not for a third part of it, and the night likewise. And I beheld, and heard an angel flying through the midst of heaven, saying with a loud voice, Woe, woe, woe, to the inhabiters of the earth by reason of the other voices of the trumpet of the three angels, which are yet to sound!

Verse 12 speaks of a plague of darkness. God used darkness at several key points in his history of redemption (Exod. 10:21–23; Joel 2:2; Mark 13:24). The first four trumpets systematically unravel God's work of creation in Genesis 1. The fourth judgment affects the sun and stars. Not only will the light diminish, but it appears that the day and night cycle will be shortened. In Joel 2:10 a plague of locusts darkened the sun and the moon.

In verse 13, we read of a woe. "Woe", in this verse, is translated in the Greek as "a terror". We see also in the Greek the term "angel" is also translated "eagle". This gives the reader a sense of meaning that this could very well be one of the four living creatures, and indicates that God may have used them also in the opening of the seven seals. These would be the three "terrors" or "woes" (8:13; see 9:12; 11:14). The cosmic signs of 8:12–13 recall the words of Amos 8:9 and of Luke 21:25.

Revelation 9:12 One woe is past; and, behold, there come two woes more hereafter.

Revelation 11:14 The second woe is past; and, behold, the third woe cometh quickly.

Amos 8:9 And it shall come to pass in that day, saith the Lord GOD, that I will cause the sun to go down at noon, and I will darken the earth in the clear day:

Luke 21:25 And there shall be signs in the sun, and in the moon, and in the stars; and upon the earth distress of nations, with perplexity; the sea and the waves roaring.

Revelation 9

***Revelation 9:1-12** The fifth trumpet- The first woe- The Plague of the Locusts-*

Revelation 9:1-12 "And the fifth angel sounded, and I saw a star fall from heaven unto the earth: and to him was given the key of the bottomless pit. And he opened the bottomless pit; and there arose a smoke out of the pit, as the smoke of a great furnace; and the sun and the air were darkened by reason of the smoke of the pit. And there came out of the smoke locusts upon the earth: and unto them was given power, as the scorpions of the earth have power. And it was commanded them that they should not hurt the grass of the earth, neither any green thing, neither any tree; but only those men which have not the seal of God in their foreheads. And to them it was given that they should not kill them, but that they should be tormented five months: and their torment was as the torment of a scorpion, when he striketh a man. And in those days shall men seek death, and shall not find it; and shall desire to die, and death shall flee from them. And the shapes of the locusts were like unto horses prepared unto battle; and on their heads were as it were crowns like gold, and their faces were as the faces of men. And they had hair as the hair of women, and their teeth were as the teeth of lions. And they

had breastplates, as it were breastplates of iron; and the
sound of their wings was as the sound of chariots of many
horses running to battle. And they had tails like unto
scorpions, and there were stings in their tails: and their
power was to hurt men five months. And they had a king
over them, which is the angel of the bottomless pit, whose
name in the Hebrew tongue is Abaddon, but in the Greek
tongue hath his name Apollyon. One woe is past; and,
behold, there come two woes more hereafter."

What is this "star fallen from heaven"?. Notice, the star is
referred to by the masculine pronoun "he". This would make
the reader think of the Old Testament and how the term star
was used to describe an angel.

**Job 38:7 When the morning stars sang together, and all the
sons of God shouted for joy?**

This same star is recorded again, in Revelation 20.

**Revelation 20:1-3 And I saw an angel come down from
heaven, having the key of the bottomless pit and a great
chain in his hand. And he laid hold on the dragon, that old
serpent, which is the Devil, and Satan, and bound him a
thousand years, And cast him into the bottomless pit, and
shut him up, and set a seal upon him, that he should
deceive the nations no more, till the thousand years should
be fulfilled: and after that he must be loosed a little season.**

The bottomless pit is not hell or hades but an underworld.
Hollis Gause writes, in his commentary, that this is the first of
the attacks on man itself. The locusts have scorpion like stings.

God has a twofold purpose in this judgment. First, to bring judgment on the world order and proving that they are powerless without him in control. Second, to make the most drastic appeal to repent.[76]

But notice their reaction,

Revelation 9:20 And the rest of the men which were not killed by these plagues yet repented not of the works of their hands, that they should not worship devils, and idols of gold, and silver, and brass, and stone, and of wood: which neither can see, nor hear, nor walk:

Revelation 9:13-19 The Sixth Trumpet- Angels and Horsemen

Revelation 9:13-19 And the sixth angel sounded, and I heard a voice from the four horns of the golden altar which is before God, Saying to the sixth angel which had the trumpet, Loose the four angels which are bound in the great river Euphrates. And the four angels were loosed, which were prepared for an hour, and a day, and a month, and a year, for to slay the third part of men. And the number of the army of the horsemen were two hundred thousand: and I heard the number of them. And thus I saw the horses in the vision, and them that sat on them, having breastplates of fire, and of jacinth, and brimstone: and the heads of the horses were as the heads of lions; and out of their mouths issued fire and smoke and brimstone. By these three was the third part of men killed, by the fire, and by the smoke, and by the brimstone, which issued out of their mouths. For their power is in their mouth, and in their tails: for their tails were like unto serpents, and had heads, and with them they do hurt.

---

[76] Gause, 109

Verse 13 reminds the hearers of the altar and the prayers of the saints in previous passages. (6:9, 8:3).

The passive participle, found in verse 14, suggests a perfect tense. Any time you see the perfect tense in the Greek, it represents a continuous action. This means that these four angels were bound and continued to be bound until the time for the wrath to be carried out.

Verses 15-16 show almost a transition or even, as one commentator states, a transformation into these four angels becoming a massive army. This army attributes to 1/3 of men being killed.[77]

Revelation 9:20-21

They still did not repent of their works. This shows the hardened hearts of men.

Revelation 10
Revelation 10:1-7

This section brings another interlude just as the gap between the sixth and seventh seals (6-8).

There are three events produced in this passage:
o The Little Book
o The Measuring of the Temple
o The Two Witnesses

The mention here of a rainbow causes the reader to think of the covenant that was made with Noah. The term "face as of the sun" reminds the reader of the Abrahamic Covenant, as well as the Davidic Covenant.

The feet of fire would remind the reader of the New Testament. So, now, in the very first verse we see nearly every

---

[77] Voorhis, 45

major covenant represented. This is a mighty angel that was sent to remind people of the covenants God had made.

Genesis 9:12-13 "And God said, This *is* the token of the covenant which I make between me and you and every living creature that *is* with you, for perpetual generations: I do set my bow in the cloud, and it shall be for a token of a covenant between me and the earth."

Genesis 12:1-3 Now the LORD had said unto Abram, Get thee out of thy country, and from thy kindred, and from thy father's house, unto a land that I will shew thee: And I will make of thee a great nation, and I will bless thee, and make thy name great; and thou shalt be a blessing: And I will bless them that bless thee, and curse him that curseth thee: and in thee shall all families of the earth be blessed."

Samuel 16:11-13 And Samuel said unto Jesse, Are here all *thy* children? And he said, there remaineth yet the youngest, and, behold, he keepeth the sheep. And Samuel said unto Jesse, Send and fetch him: for we will not sit down till he come hither. And he sent, and brought him in. Now he *was* ruddy, *and* withal of a beautiful countenance, and goodly to look to. And the LORD said, Arise, anoint him: for this *is* he. Then Samuel took the horn of oil, and anointed him in the midst of his brethren: and the Spirit of the LORD came upon David from that day forward. So, Samuel rose up, and went to Ramah.

(Notice that David was in the sun, doing the Father's business at his call.)

The Seven Thunders- "Write them not"

Remarkably interesting is this stretch of text. The truth is

That no one really knows what these seven thunders are. Dr. Voorhis, in his commentary, says we can assume that they could be some plagues just as the seven seals, trumpets, and vials are.[78]

Revelation 10:8-11 *John is commanded to Eat the Little Book*

The eating of this book has several possible meanings. It is reminiscent of the similar experience Ezekiel had, in Ezekiel, chapter 2.

Ezekiel 2:9-10 And when I looked, behold, an hand *was* sent unto me; and, lo, a roll of a book *was* therein; And he spread it before me; and it *was* written within and without: and *there was* written therein lamentations, and mourning, and woe.

Ezekiel 3:1-3 Moreover he said unto me, Son of man, eat that thou findest; eat this roll, and go speak unto the house of Israel. So I opened my mouth, and he caused me to eat that roll. And he said unto me, Son of man, cause thy belly to eat, and fill thy bowels with this roll that I give thee. Then did I eat *it*; and it was in my mouth as honey for sweetness. [79]

Larkin, in his commentary, says that this could be the same book that is mentioned in Daniel 12[80]

Daniel 12:4 "But thou, O Daniel, shut up the words, and seal the book, *even* to the time of the end: many shall run to and fro, and knowledge shall be increased."

---

[78] Voorhis, 45

[79] Voorhis, 45

[80] Larkin, 81

Whichever position it is, we can see it is a little book. And just like the Word of God it is sweet to taste but bitter in judgment.

After this John is told to prophesy again during the Apocalypse.

Revelation 11

Revelation 11:1-2

We begin this section with what this author sees as the climax of this book, as it relates to those of us who are part of the modern Pentecostal movement. There is so much in this chapter that we can draw from, that relates to us today.

The Greek translation of verse one, in the Interlinear, is translated "GET UP AND MEASURE THE SANCTUARY OF GOD AND THE ALTER AND THOSE WHO WORSHIP IN IT." This points us to the of Old and New Testament references to measuring the temple:

- Ezekiel 40-42
- Zech. 2:1-5
- Matthew 21:12-13

Notice here John is told to measure three things:

- The Temple
- The Altar
- The Worshippers

Some hold this to be a temple that is yet to be rebuilt and refers to the same temple that the Anti-Christ will be in. However, there are some that would hold this is a symbol of the people of God, due to the Greek rendering of Sanctuary.[81]

I feel it is both. This is due to the fact of the already and not yet kingdom of God. As the "already", we are to measure

---

[81] Waddell,165-166

up to God with the altar and worship. As the "not yet", we have not seen the rebuilding of this temple, but we know it will be, due to the fact the Anti-Christ will reign.

Verse 2 reveals a powerful prophecy, in that the outer court is given to be tread upon by the gentiles, while the altar and worshippers are in the inner court. This is, to me, part of the fulfillment of previous New Testament prophecies. The outer court is the form.

2 Timothy 3:5 "Having a form of godliness but denying the power thereof: from such turn away."

2 Timothy 4:3 "For the time will come when they will not endure sound doctrine; but after their own lusts shall they heap to themselves teachers, having itching ears."

Can I tell you, we are seeing the prelude to this, even now? Just look at the recent events in the Pentecostal Movement and even in Christianity in general.

- The shift in the paradigm from inter-denominational to inter-faith.
- The decline in the Baptism of the Holy Spirit which is becoming like third century Christianity.
- The acceptance of the immorality of 2 Timothy 3:1-5.
- The doctrinal corruption that has been contributed by Neo-Pentecostal Movements such as the Charismatic, Reformed Charismatic, etc.

The Two Witnesses

The Story of the two witnesses can be divided as follows:

- The prophetic testimony of the two witnesses.
- The attack of the beast and the death of the witnesses.

- The resurrection and ascension of the two witnesses.
- The earthquake judgment[82]

Revelation 11:3-6

In Verse 3, the wearing of sackcloth symbolizes the writings, in the Old Testament of Joel, and the attire of the prophets such as Elijah and John the Baptist (Joel 1-2, 2 Kings 1:8, Mark 1:6). Jewish scholars record sackcloth as both a symbol of mourning and repentance.

The meaning we draw, as the church of today, is that until the return of Jesus, we must continue to mourn over the lost, while delivering a message of repentance.

For the literal interpretation of this text, the two witnesses are bringing hope amid the wrath of the Lamb. Even after the unrepentant hearts of those in chapter 9, there is still yet hope.

In Verse 4, the two olive trees give symbolic meaning in this text. The olive tree was significant in the anointing oil, and these two witnesses are the two anointed ones, which literal interpretation deems sons of oil who stand on the earth.

This reminds the reader of a past revelation of the two olive trees in Zech. 4:14.

Zechariah 4:14 " Then said he, these *are* the two anointed ones, that stand by the Lord of the whole earth."

It is widely accepted in the Zechariah account that the two olive trees were Joshua and Zerubabbal. Given the relationship here between the two experiences of the olive trees, there is also the lampstand which is a symbol of the Holy Spirit.

---

[82] Waddell, 170

Zechariah 4:10 "For who hath despised the day of small things? for they shall rejoice, and shall see the plummet in the hand of Zerubbabel *with* those seven; they *are* the eyes of the LORD, which run to and fro through the whole earth."

What makes this more interesting about the Zechariah vision with the lampstand, he mentions **"...the plummet in the hand of Zerubbabel *with* those seven"**. Then, here in Revelation 11, John refers to the seven lamps, as he is referencing Christ and the Seven Churches.[83]

My observation from this research shows me a couple of things. The eschatological community we are in of Pre-Millennialism can take it several ways.

➤ For the Pre-Tribulationist position, it can be easily said that the lampstand (the church) is taken out because the two olive trees are the only ones mentioned in the text.
➤ For the Mid-Tribulationist position, the lampstand is canonically connected with this text, and Zechariah gives the fact that the first olive tree is present. The lampstand is taken out before the second olive tree comes. Thus, creating a first witness in the first half of the tribulation and a second witness.
➤ For the Post-Tribulationist position, this connection gives an argument for the church being in the tribulation due to the olive trees getting their witness from the lampstand.

(It is my understanding that this verse is best supported by the pre-tribulation position given the lack of the lampstand being mentioned in the text.)

Verses 5-6 reveal a supernatural power that these witnesses have. This is a direct fulfillment of the promises

---

[83] Waddell172-174

given, both in Mark 16 and in the Book of Acts, of signs following the believer.

Revelation 11:7-10

The beast is mentioned here which is also known in Eschatological circles as the Anti-Christ. The unique thing about this verse is that the beast is recorded in Revelation 12-13 as coming on the scene. That would place this passage out of chronological sequence.

Koester in his commentary has a chart that shows that Revelation is more circular than straight-line. The chart he uses, in his book, goes literally in circles and when you think you have an ending, it is just beginning.

The beast kills the witnesses. Nothing new here because of what John 10:10 says.

It is here that some scholars interpret the two witnesses as Enoch and Elijah. Their reasoning is because these two did not see death.

Another unique aspect of this passage is the place where they died. They died where the Lord was crucified.

Three days and a half they lie dead in the streets. And the attitude of the world is one of celebration and mockery.

Revelation 11:11-12

God raised them up through the agency of the Holy Spirit-"The Spirit of Life". Great fear fell upon those that saw this. The fact that the Holy Spirit is the agent of life in creation, raising up of our Lord, and our new life in Christ.[84]

Genesis 2:7 " And the LORD God formed man *of* the dust of the ground and breathed into his nostrils the breath of life; and man became a living soul."

---

[84] Gause, 154-155

Romans 1:4 And declared *to be* the Son of God with power, according to the spirit of holiness, by the resurrection from the dead:"

John 3:5-6 "Jesus answered, Verily, verily, I say unto thee, except a man be born of water and *of* the Spirit, he cannot enter into the kingdom of God. That which is born of the flesh is flesh; and that which is born of the Spirit is spirit."

Titus 3:5 "Not by works of righteousness which we have done, but according to his mercy he saved us, by the washing of regeneration, and renewing of the Holy Ghost."

Like Christ, they are taken up to heaven. This reminds the reader of the hope of Christ taking us away.

1 Thessalonians 4:16-18 "For the Lord himself shall descend from heaven with a shout, with the voice of the archangel, and with the trump of God: and the dead in Christ shall rise first: Then we which are alive *and* remain shall be caught up together with them in the clouds, to meet the Lord in the air: and so shall we ever be with the Lord. Wherefore comfort one another with these words."

Revelation 11:13

A unique part of this judgment is when seven thousand men died. Could this very well be the very ones who were celebrating in the previous verses?

This earthquake is unique, in that it ushers in a worship scene which is carried on the preceding verses along with judgment.

Revelation 11:15-19 "And the seventh angel sounded; and there were great voices in heaven, saying, The kingdoms of this world are become *the kingdoms* of our Lord, and of his Christ; and he shall reign for ever and ever. And the four and twenty elders, which sat before God on their seats, fell upon their faces, and worshipped God, Saying, We give thee thanks, O Lord God Almighty, which art, and wast, and art to come; because thou hast taken to thee thy great power, and hast reigned. And the nations were angry, and thy wrath is come, and the time of the dead, that they should be judged, and that thou shouldest give reward unto thy servants the prophets, and to the saints, and them that fear thy name, small and great; and shouldest destroy them which destroy the earth. And the temple of God was opened in heaven, and there was seen in his temple the ark of his testament: and there were lightnings, and voices, and thundering, and an earthquake, and great hail."

Revelation 12

Revelation 12:1-6 The Woman and the Dragon

This is the second reference to a woman in the book of Revelation. The first reference of course was used negatively in the Seven Churches with Jezebel.

Revelation 2:20-23 "Notwithstanding I have a few things against thee, because thou sufferest that woman Jezebel, which calleth herself a prophetess, to teach and to seduce my servants to commit fornication, and to eat things sacrificed unto idols. And I gave her space to repent of her fornication; and she repented not. Behold, I will cast her into a bed, and them that commit adultery with her into great tribulation, except they repent of their deeds. And I will kill her children with death; and all the churches shall know that I am he which searcheth the reins and

hearts: and I will give unto every one of you according to your works."

This woman though shows a picture of cosmic loyalty, power, and promise.

Her description and location give proximity to God. She had the sun and moon under her feet to show her dominion. She gave birth to a man-child who was going to rule the earth with a rod of iron.[85]

Voorhis, in his commentary, lists three prominent theories suggesting who this woman is:

- o Woman represents the Virgin Mary. This theory is held by the Catholic Church.
- o The post-tribulation position hold that this woman is the church and the man-child is the overcomes.
- o The most prominent theory is that the Woman is Israel and the man-child is Jesus.[86]

The theory of the man-child Jesus is supported by the following arguments:

- o Christ came out of the Nation of Israel -Psalm 2:9
- o The Devil tried to destroy Christ as soon as He was born- Matthew 2:16
- o Christ was caught up to God and His throne- Acts 1:9

However, Dr. Voorhis points out that if you hold a chronological order to the book, this theory is more toward another idea, of the man-child being the 144,000 Jews. He supports the argument by:

- o Chronological order
- o 144,000 caught up to God
- o Israel's children are Jewish

---

[85] Thomas, 404-407

[86] Voorhis, 52

- o Promise to overcomers in Revelation 2:26-27
- o Israel would produce a remnant that would be delivered from the time of Jacob's trouble.[87]

The personal view of this author is that the nation of Israel is the woman and Jesus is the man-child.

Revelation is not in chronological order. For example, the beast appears in Revelation 11 but does not come on the scene until Revelation 13.

The 144,000 are caught up to God, but I do not think they fight in heaven. Revelation 12:1-6 is more of a prophetic history on how we got to the time of the apocalypse.

The child (singular) was going to rule with a rod of iron. This, no doubt, signifies the prophetic promise of Christ.

Revelation 12:7-8 War in Heaven

Michael is known as one of the archangels.

Jude 1:9 "Yet Michael the archangel, when contending with the devil he disputed about the body of Moses, durst not bring against him a railing accusation, but said, The Lord rebuke thee."

This war is fought in Heaven with Michael. Michael and war were a common theme in the Word of God. He brings a deliverance to those who are written in the book of Life.

Daniel 12:1 "And at that time shall Michael stand up, the great prince which standeth for the children of thy people: and there shall be a time of trouble, such as never was since

---

[87] Voorhis, 55

there was a nation *even* to that same time: and at that time thy people shall be delivered, every one that shall be found written in the book."

Michael helped Daniel overcome opposition.

Daniel 10:13 "But the prince of the kingdom of Persia withstood me one and twenty days: but, lo, Michael, one of the chief princes, came to help me; and I remained there with the kings of Persia."

Daniel 10:21 "But I will shew thee that which is noted in the scripture of truth: and *there is* none that holdeth with me in these things, but Michael your prince."

The voice of the archangel will accompany the return of Jesus Christ[88]

1 Thessalonians 4:16-17 "For the Lord himself shall descend from heaven with a shout, with the voice of the archangel, and with the trump of God: and the dead in Christ shall rise first: Then we which are alive *and* remain shall be caught up together with them in the clouds, to meet the Lord in the air: and so shall we ever be with the Lord."

Revelation 12:9-11 The Identity of the Dragon

Verse 9 identifies the dragon as the Devil. The term "Devil", rendered here in the Greek, is slanderer and is also supported by Him being called, in this text, the accuser of the brethren.

---

[88] Gause, 168

In the verses following we see how that the enemy was overcome:

- He was cast out of heaven
- Worship rang out
- They overcame the enemy by
- The blood of the lamb
- Word of their testimony
- Loved not their lives unto the death

Revelation 12:13-17 *The Dragon on Earth*

The dragon continued to attack the woman. Now, here is where it gets interesting.

Notice the earth (Gentiles) swallowed up the woman. This symbolizes the grafting of the vine between the Church and Israel.

Keep in mind that this is a prophetic history, which sets the stage for the remainder of the book. John was recording this history to show how the Beast (Anti-Christ) was going to come about.

The Bible records that we would suffer persecution for living Godly. Right now, we are in spiritual warfare (Ephesians 6).

So, now the stage is set for the Anti-Christ to come on the scene. Notice the promise given in verse 12. He has only a short time. Even amid all this attack on God's people, it will only last a season.

Revelation 13
Revelation 13:1-10

We begin to see here a beast appear. What is amazing is that the beast is just coming on the scene here, but he is also in Revelation, chapter 11.

The Beast is empowered by the Dragon, which we know from Revelation 12, to be the devil. Thus, the Anti-Christ has come on the scene.

With the image speaking in the temple, we now have a Satanic Trinity.

Names for the Anti-Christ throughout the Word of God:

Old Testament

- The Assyrian- Isaiah 10:5-6, Isaiah 30:27-33
- The King of Babylon- Isaiah 14:4
- The Little Horn- Daniel 7:8, Daniel 8:9-12
- A King of fierceness- Daniel 8:23
- The prince that shall come- Daniel 9:26
- The Willful King- Daniel 11:36

New Testament

- The Man of Sin
- The Son of Perdition
- That Wicked- 2 Thes. 2:3-8
- The Antichrist- 1 John 2:18
- The Beast- Rev. 13:1-2[89]
- The Person of the Anti-Christ
- Persuasive speaker- Rev 13:5-6
- Military Genius Rev 13:4,7
- Political Leader
- Totally Egocentric- Daniel 11:36-37

The anti-Christ establishes his own religious system over the worlds system, according to Revelation 13:8, Revelation 13:14-15, and 2 Thessalonians 2:4.

---

[89] Voorhis, 57-92

The Power of the Antichrist

- 2 Thesssalonians 2:9-10
- Revelation 13:2
- 1 John 2:18
- Revelation 13:13-17

The power he demonstrates shows that he is to be the Spirit of Prophecy for this trinity of evil.

He uses this power for these purposes:

- He causes people on the earth to worship the beast- v.12
- He performs great signs- v.13-14
- These signs have the appearance of miracles
- He represents in the evil realm the power and victory over death- v.15-17[90]
- His Ministry gives the Antichrist Power- Rev. 13:11-15
- His Ministry establishes the mark of the beast- Rev. 13:16-18

At the conclusion of this text, in verse 16-18, we read of a mark of the beast. For years, I have heard the number 666. However, in my research of other texts—specifically, the Greek New Testament, The New Revised Standard Version, and New American—I have found that some earlier manuscripts of the New Testament actually render this number to be 616.

Regardless of the number we know that it is received on either the right hand or the forehead. Given the language in the book of Revelation, we can read that the right hand and forehead both symbolize the authority of God (Rev. 2-3, 5). Thus, the Satanic Trinity is making total mockery, now, of not only God, but the people of God. He started with the image in the temple but now there is the mark.

---

[90] Gause, 183-184

Schools of thought emerge on this mark. Some believe that this mark is something like a microchip that will be inserted. Some hold this as a symbol of the loyalty of those to the Anti-Christ. Whatever position one holds, the reality of it is true. There will be a mockery of God, His place of worship, and people during this time.

Revelation 14

Revelation 14:1-5

This passage of scripture centers around two senses of John, the author. First, it centers around what John sees in verse 1. Then, in verses 2-5, it centers around what he hears.

What he sees is the Lamb standing on Mount Zion. Then he sees the 144,000, which were mentioned in Revelation 7. He then hears two things: *Heavenly harps* (14:2) and *Heavenly hosannas* (14:3–5): The 144,000 now sing a song no one else can sing.[91]

In verse 1, he left the heavenly position which is given here in this verse by saying: having left His position "in the midst of the throne," and now taking His stand *"on Sion"*.[92] This gives the full authority of the Lamb, not only in heaven, but now on earth.

Scholars argue that now the "GREAT TRIBULATION" begins, or the last 3 ½ years as dispensationalists argue.

In verse 2-3 we see a new song being sung. They have a new song to sing that others cannot share (see Ps. 33:3; 40:3;

---

[91]Willmington, H. L.: *The Outline Bible.* Wheaton, Ill. : Tyndale House Publishers, 1999, S. Re 14:2-5

[92]Jamieson, Robert ; Fausset, A. R. ; Fausset, A. R. ; Brown, David ; Brown, David: *A Commentary, Critical and Explanatory, on the Old and New Testaments.* Oak Harbor, WA : Logos Research Systems, Inc., 1997, S. Re 14:1

96:1; 98:1; 144:9; 149:1). They are accompanied by heavenly harps and other heavenly voices.[93] This choir is singing, it seems, both in the heavens and on earth.

The only ones that could sing this song were the redeemed! This shows the requirement of the song. It is not an elegant voice, a wonderful pitch, or an awesome talent, but it is the fact that we are redeemed by the blood of Jesus Christ.

The usage here of not being defiled with women, basically I feel, is symbolic with the reoccurring theme of the worldliness in the church such as the Jezebelic Spirit in Revelation 3, and the worldly church that is recorded in Revelation 11.

Without fault before the throne of God shows the goal of the redeemed. This reminds us of the passage in the Gospels, found in Matthew 25:21, where scripture records "well done, thou good and faithful servant."

Revelation 14:6-20

In this stretch of text, we have three angelic messages.

First, there is the Gospel being preached in verses 6-7. But notice here the term is everlasting Gospel. The term here for everlasting is αἰώνιον meaning an eternal Gospel. The same message of redemption from the beginning in Genesis is now being fulfilled in Revelation.

Second, there is the message of Babylon falling, found in verse 8. This is the first prophetic utterance of what will transpire in Revelation 18. The reader would also recount the passage in Revelation 16:18-19 where reflection is given to the fall of Babylon. Scholars are mixed when it comes to this account. Some hold this as a symbol of the economic system of the Anti-Christ while some hold it as a literal Babylon being

---

[93]Wiersbe, Warren W.: *The Bible Exposition Commentary*. Wheaton, Ill. : Victor Books, 1996, c1989, S. Re 14:1

built. Those who hold this as the governmental economic system of the Anti-Christ also tend to hold the Great Whore of Babylon as the religious system of the Anti-Christ. This is, no doubt, warranted by the fact that the previous terminology of women in the earlier verses of this chapter also produces grounds to support the argument for the great whore being a religious system.

Third there is the message of "do not worship the beast nor receive its mark", in verse 9. The consequences of this can be seen in the following verses, as a prophetic utterance given to what awaits at the battle of Armageddon, and before that, the wrath of God.

Verses 10-13 give the ultimatum here of either being touched by the Lamb of God or face the wrath of the Lamb of God. This wrath, no doubt, refers not just to the wrath of the Lamb, thus far, but the final stages of the wrath of the Lamb that leads up to Armageddon.

Verses 14-20 give the preview of the battle of Armageddon which is recorded in Revelation 16.

Revelation 15
Revelation 15:1-8

In the first verse, we read the phrase "and I saw". This indicates that something new is about to take place in the vision.

Verse 2 shows the overcoming element they have. They are standing on a sea of glass. And in that glass, they see the sea mingled with fire. The term for fire here denotes the wrath of the lamb as previously stated earlier in the study. Once again, it denotes the same Greek term for fire, which is *puri*. This is the same term used in Matthew 3:11. This fire is the wrath of the Lamb.

Verse 3 denotes the two songs being sung. They are The

Song of Moses and of the Lamb. Here shows the completion of the Old and New Covenants. The relationship here expands the terminology of the already and not yet kingdom of God. The already here is the song of Moses which is found in Exodus 15:1-21 and the not yet begins to take shape. McGee, in his commentary, points out that this shows God to be the King of the Ages, while the rest of the book of Revelation shows him King of nations, tribes, and peoples.

Verse 4 denotes a constant theme in the Apocalypse worship accompanied by judgement. This theme is seen throughout the Apocalypse, in Revelation 7, during the seven seals, in Revelation 11 with the two witnesses, and now here in Revelation 15.

The tabernacle being opened in heaven, in verse 5, and the accompaniment of the smoke and manifestations of the Glory of God being there, shows that there is worship in the temple, even during the time of great wrath.

It is interesting to note the term smoke here, which in the Greek is *kapnou*. This is the same Greek word used, in Revelation 8:4, as the smoke which accompanied the incense of the prayers of the saints. This shows that even in the final hour, intercession is still being made for souls to get right before God. The fact that this continues, until the plagues are fulfilled, denotes such intercession.

Revelation 16
Revelation 16:1-7

We see here, in the first verse, permission given to the angels to pour their vials or, as the Greek translate, bowls upon the earth.

This vial judgment reminds us of the sixth plague in Egypt (Ex. 9:8-12; note also Deut. 28:27, 35). Only those who have submitted to "the beast" and who have rejected the warning of the first angel will experience this judgment (Rev. 14:6-7).

Revelation 16:10-11 suggests that these sores do not disappear; for by the time of the fifth vial, people are still in pain from the first judgment. Yet their pain will not cause them to repent (see Rev. 9:20-21). William R. Newell used to say, "If men are not won by grace, they will never be won." It is an awesome thought to consider almost the entire population of the world suffering from a painful malady that nothing can cure. Constant pain affects a person's disposition, so that he finds it difficult to get along with other people. Human relations during that period will certainly be at their worst.[94]

Verse 3 deals with the sea and blood. J. Vernon McGee's commentary holds that blood is the token of life. "For the life of the flesh is in the blood . . ." (Lev. 17:11). The sea is a great reservoir of life. It is teeming with life, and the salty water is a cathartic for the filth of the earth.

However, in this plague, blood is the token of death; the sea becomes a grave of death instead of a womb of life. The cool sea breezes become a stench from the carcasses floating on the surface of the bloody water and lining the shore. Commerce is paralyzed. Human beings died like flies. The first plague in Egypt was the turning of the waters of the Nile River into blood (see Exod. 7:20-25). There is a striking similarity here.[95]

Verse 4 deals with the water supply again. This affects all remaining bodies of water not mentioned in the previous texts.

According to Voorhis' commentary, this sets the stage for Armageddon, for if the water to blood plague is on all the bodies of water rather than those in the territory of the Anti-Christ, the earth can no longer endure.

---

[94]Wiersbe, Warren W.: *The Bible Exposition Commentary*. Wheaton, Ill. : Victor Books, 1996, c1989, S. Re 14:1

[95] J. Vernon McGee: *Thru the Bible with J. Vernon McGee*, Copyright 1983,Thomas Nelson, Inc., Nashville

It is believed by many scholars that these plagues are in sequence of one another and that verses14-16 suggest the preparation for Armageddon.[96]

Verses 5-7 give a sense of worship during judgment. When one hears the waters cry out, one can think of either the pain of death in the water, or worship to God because the wrath.

Verses 6-7 shows us that the latter is to be taken as what is going on.

Revelation 16:8-16

We get to another point in the Apocalypse here, where the writer gives us a reaction to the judgments from those inhabitants on the earth. What strikes me here is the manifestations of Chapter 11, the everlasting Gospel of Chapter 14, and the wrath of the Lamb here in Chapter 16 is being poured in its most severe measure. Yet, there is still no sign of repentance, but in verse 9 and 11 we see the term ἐβλασφήμησαν. This would suggest an aorist tense in third person plural. This indicates that a multitude, rather than one person, is blaspheming God here. The expected situation would have been repentance, but instead, there was the opposite, total rebellion.

In verse 15, we find a saying, "Behold, I come as a thief". This saying should not surprise the hearers because canonically it is a phrase Paul used to describe the coming of the Lord, in 1 Thess. 5. Peter also used this terminology, in 2 Peter 3. However, in the Apocalypse, Jesus uses this saying to describe His return in Revelation 3:3.

In Verse 16, we see the gathering beginning to take place for the battle of Armageddon. The word "Armageddon" occurs only in Revelation 16:16 (R.V., "Har-Magedon"), as

---

[96] Voorhis, 97

symbolically designating the place where the "battle of that great day of God Almighty" (Rev. 14) shall be fought. The word properly means the "mount of Megiddo." It is the scene of the final conflict between Christ and Antichrist. The idea of such a scene was suggested by the Old Testament great battlefield, the plain of Esdraelon.[97]

Revelation 16:17-21

In this passage, we read a completion of the wrath by saying it is done.

In verse 18, we read of a great earthquake that divided the city of the nations, and that every island fled away and there were no mountains found. The reaction to the wrath's completion, by those who experienced it, is still blasphemy. So, with the destruction of the city comes the destruction of the political and religious systems yet to be discussed.

---

[97]Matthew George Easton: Easton's Illustrated Bible Dictionary: Electronic Edition, Ephihamy Software, 1995

4

IN THE SPIRIT CARRIED TO THE WILDERNESS: *REVELATION 17-22:9*

Revelation 17

Revelation 17:1-5

At first, one reads the description of this woman, and can immediately think of previous texts in the Apocalypse of Jezebel. The term fornication which is used many times suggests either an adulterous or presumptuous relationship outside the plan of marriage. When one looks at it in this perspective, perhaps it makes sense to note that we, as the church, are referred to as the Bride of Christ in Revelation 19 and again in chapter 22. Given this note, the harlot here could very well be representative of the one world religious system that the beast is establishing.

The description of this woman, as it relates to her attire, gives yet another support of the above argument. The fact that both the beast in verse three, and the woman in verse four, are clothed identically, give an identity of relationship to one another. It is indeed the beast that empowers this mockery of a religious system, in that in verse three she sat upon it and rode it.

In verse 4, there is another clue given with the abominations in her hand. This term is also used by Jesus in the Synoptic Gospels when He speaks of the abomination of desolation. The term for this in the Greek is βδελυγμάτων in which the root is used six times to indicate idolatry and desolation.[98]

So, with this evidence one can conclude that this is the one world religious system that is empowered by the beast and worshipped by those who receive his mark.

Revelation 17:5-9

The intention, here in this passage, is to begin by verse 5 to identify a relationship between her name and character. The symbolism here that John portrays is borrowed from Roman culture.

Prostitutes in Rome wore a headdress with the name harlot on it. The relationship here shows two things. First, the seal of God is upon the forehead of the people as seen earlier in the Apocalypse. Second, the mark of the beast was on the right hand or forehead of its followers, thus is the case here. The term mystery here is by implication a spiritual nature.[99] Just as this term "mystery" is used in Christian circles concerning eschatology, in this circle the same can be said.

Verse 6 gives the statement of persecution the harlot did to the saints of God. This is seen throughout the apocalypse, including the souls under the altar in Revelation 6, the death of the two witnesses in Revelation 11, and also the beheading

---

[98] Strong, Strong's Concordinance, Electronic Ed.

[99] Gause, 221-222

of believers in Revelation 20:4. In observing this, I feel the groundwork to this harlot's mission is laid in Revelation 3 with the Jezebelic Spirit.

Verses 7-9 show the relationship the one world religious system has with the one world government. This is really brought out in verse 9.

The sitting on a mountain theme is no new theme to the hearers. In the Gospels, we read of Jesus' temptation and the devil taking him on top of a mountain. We then read this theme again here.

Revelation 17:9-11

This verse gives an interesting aspect to the identity of the beast. Some scholars argue that this represents a turning against the harlot with the eleventh verses usage of perdition which in the Greek is translated destruction. However, if one takes the whole text of Revelation into consideration this reflects the wound on the head of the beast that was spoken of as early as Genesis 3:15.

Nevertheless, now that the religious system is crumbling, we are beginning to see everything else crumble as well. This is symbolic, now, of the economic collapse of the kingdom of the Anti-Christ or the beast.

Revelation 17:12-18

Verse 12 gives us a description of the ten horns which was also discussed in Revelation 12 with the dragon. These are the nations by which the beast runs the one world order with. The terminology here of one hour can also be translated in the Greek text μιαν ὡραν, one time, (as it may be properly translated), i.e., at the same time with the beast, or that which ascend out of the bottomless pit.

Verse 13 shows that this government gives power to the beast, and the beast as stated earlier gave power to the harlot. Thus, the relationship lies between the beast, its government, economy, and religion.

Verse 14 is of known fact that this refers to Armageddon.

Verses 15-18 show that the systems turn on each other, and thus, it gives the underlying of not only the beast being defeated by the Lamb, but the very things that made the beast powerful as well.

Revelation 18

The events of Revelation 18 are viewed as a song of reflection from the events in Revelation 17.

The term is fallen is repeated quite a bit in the text. This gives the sense of the awesome destruction that took place in Revelation 17.

The third verse gives an account of the nations partaking with her, even though she is destroyed or is being destroyed. The symbolism here of harlotry often is used, in the Canon, to depict corrupted religious practices.

Verse 4 is a scripture that the post-tribulation view uses to argue their view of the rapture, because here we are at the end, and a voice is saying come up hither.

Verses 5-8 deal with the curse of sin, and the solution as it related to the Lord.

A series of songs of defeat comprise this song. Notice this song's main object of mourning is not just the city but the materialism in the city.

It is interesting to note hear who sings the songs of defeat. They are the rulers of the world (18:9-10), the merchants (18:11-16), and the ship owners (18:17-20). These have all grown rich because of the evil economy, representative of

Babylon. The fall of the evil world system will affect all who enjoyed and depended on it. No one will remain unaffected by Babylon's fall.

There are three groups in this fall:

First, the rulers who had given their power to the beast had committed immoral acts with her. As a reward for their subservience, these kings enjoyed her great luxury. But when the city is destroyed, they will be terrified by her great torment and will stand at a distance. Most likely, the destruction is so great that they do not want to be caught up in it. They do not attempt to rescue the city because they realize it is futile. These rulers will be terrified because, without Babylon, they will be nothing. They are terrified for Babylon, but more important, they are terrified for themselves.

Second, there are the merchants (18:11-16). These people weep and mourn because there is no one left to buy their goods. The collapse of the economy will mean the end of their trade and income.

The third group to join the funeral dirge will be the ship owners and captains of the merchant ships and their crews—all who earn their living from the sea.

Revelation 19
Revelation 19:1-6

"Our God", declared in verse 1, shows whose God is being declared.

In Verse 2, four "Alleluias" are introduced.

o Salvation
o Glory
o Honor
o Power

The word alleluia is translated in the Greek "hallelujah", which means, in the Old Testament, "to praise Jah" or "Praise

Jehovah", and in the New Testament is translated "Praise the Lord."

Verse 2 also addresses the destruction of the harlot.

The smoke, in verse 3, shows the demise of the false religious system, which is permanent.

Revelation 19:7-10

There are a number of significant things we find in this passage:

> ➢ The Savior is the Bridegroom- John 1:29.
> ➢ This preparation of the bride can be also described in Matthew 25:1-10.
> ➢ John gets tempted here to worship the angel. However, the angel says for John not to do so.
> ➢ The identity of the church as the bride completes its identity.
> o Mystery- Romans 9:25-26
> o Body- Eph 1:22-23
> o Building- Eph 2:20-22

The term of the church being virgin means it is doctrinally pure church.

Revelation 19:11-16

Heaven is still recorded as opened, in verse 11. Then, we find a tremendous description of Christ.

Verse 12 declares that He had a name no one knew.

In verse 13, Christ has a robe dipped in his own blood. This is linked to Isaiah 63:2-4

The armies of heaven followed in verse 14.

Verse 15 tells us that He rules with a rod of iron (see Psalm 2:9).

In verse 16, He is declared "King of Kings and Lord of Lords".

Revelation 19:17-21

The destruction is so great that it requires birds to clean up the battlefield. This scene is the completion of judgement on this evil and cruel world

Related passages include Revelation 14:14-20, 16:13-16, and 17:14.

Old Testament passages pointing to this include Jeremiah 51:27-44, Ezekiel 39:17-20, Joel 3:9-16, Zephaniah 3:8, and Zechariah 14:2-5.

Beginning with verse 19, war is declared. This war will end swiftly with the destruction of the Antichrist and all the ungodly, according to verses 19-21.

The Old Testament records that the judgment of God not only includes these armies but the entire world (see Jeremiah. 25:29-33).

This false prophet once again is described as one performing the signs (see Revelation 13:13-15, 2 Thessalonians 2:9-10, and Matthew 24:24).

The term "lake of fire" is only used in the book of revelation. It is a place of punishment for the beast and false prophet (verses 19:20). This is also Satan's destination (20:10). Death and hell cast into the lake of fire, which is declared to be the second death (20:14). Those whose names are not written in the book of life are also cast into it (20:15), along with the evildoers (21:8).

The remnant is then slain. This confirms the following:

- Those who reject the truth will be destroyed (2 Thessalonians 2:11-12)

- The Unrighteous will not inherit the kingdom of God (1 Corinthians. 6:9-11, Galatians 5:19-21)
- They will be separated from the righteous after Christ returns in glory and will be assigned eternal punishment (Matthew 25:31-46)

Revelation 20

Revelation 20:1-3 The Binding of Satan

An angel comes down from heaven, with the key of the bottomless pit, and a great chain in his hand, and seizes upon the dragon, and casts him into the pit, that for a thousand years he should deceive the nations no more.

The great enemy of God and his cause is thus made a prisoner and is restrained from making war in any form against the church. The way is thus prepared for the peace and triumph which follow.

Revelation 20:4-6

John sees thrones, and persons sitting on them. He sees the souls of those who were beheaded for the witness of Jesus, and for the word of God--those who had not worshipped the beast nor his image--living and reigning with Christ during the thousand years. We see the spirits of the martyrs revived, and becoming again the reigning spirit on earth. This he calls the first resurrection; and on all such he says the second death has no power.

They may experience temporal death--for such the martyrs had experienced--but over them the second death has no dominion, for they live and reign with the Savior.

This is properly the millennium—the long period when the principles of true religion will have the ascendency on the earth. The martyrs and confessors, the most devoted and eminent Christians of other times, shall appear again upon the earth. It is as if their spirit should become the reigning and pervading spirit of all who professed the Christian name.

Revelation 20:7-8

After the thousand years of peace and triumph shall have expired, Satan will be released from his prison, and will be permitted to go out and deceive the nations which are in the four quarters of the earth, and gather them together to battle; that is, a state of things will exist as if Satan were then released.

Revelation 20:9-10

After the temporary and partial outbreak of evil (Revelation 20:7, 8), Satan and his hosts will be destroyed. The destruction will be as if fire should come down from heaven to devour the assembled hosts (Revelation 20:9), and as if Satan, the great leader of evil, should be cast into the same lake where the beast and false prophet are, to be tormented forever. Then, the church will be delivered from all its enemies, and religion henceforward will be triumphant.

How long the interval will be between this state and that next disclosed as the final judgment is not stated. The eye of the seer glances from one to the other, but there is nothing to forbid the supposition, that, according to the laws of prophetic vision, there may be a long interval in which righteousness shall reign upon the earth.

Revelation 20:11-15

This closes the earthly scene. Henceforward the scene is transferred to heaven—the abode of the redeemed.

The last judgment is the winding up of the earthly affairs. The enemies of the church have all long since been destroyed;

the world has experienced, perhaps for a long series of ages, the full influence of the gospel; countless millions have been, we may suppose, brought under its power; and then at last, in the winding up of human affairs, comes the judgment of the great day, when the dead, small and great, shall stand before God; when the sea shall give up its dead; when death and hell shall give up the dead that are in them; when the records of human actions shall be opened, and all shall be judged according to their works, and when all who are not found written in the book of life shall be cast into the lake of fire. This is the earthly consummation; henceforward the saints shall reign in glory-the New Jerusalem above.

Revelation 21

Revelation 21:1-7 The Habitation of the Bride

The descent of this city is found in verses 1 and 2.

"And I saw a new heaven and a new earth: for the first heaven and the first earth were passed away; and there was no more sea" (21:1).

John here sees a new heaven and earth. Thus, between Revelation 20 and 21 the old heaven and earth is apparently destroyed.

The fact of this destruction.

"Heaven and earth shall pass away, but my words shall not pass away" (Mt. 24:35).

"Thou, Lord, in the beginning hast laid the foundation of the earth, and the heavens are the works of thine hands;

**they shall perish but thou remainest; and they shall all wax
old as doth a garment, and as a vesture shalt thou fold
them up, and they shall be changed; but thou art the same,
and thy years shall not fail" (Hebrews 1:10-12).**

**"But the day of the Lord will come as a thief in the night,
in the which the heavens shall pass away with a great noise,
and the elements shall melt with a fervent heat; the earth
also and the works that are therein shall be burned up" (2
Peter 3:10, 11).**

Verse 4 records ultimate healing.

- No More Tears
- No More Death
- No More Sorrow
- No More Crying
- No More Pain

In Verse 6, as always, Jesus invites those who are
spiritually thirsty to come to him and drink of his "living
water" (see John 7:37-39). This water relates to the life-giving
quality of the Holy Spirit through spiritual salvation, the
baptism in the Holy Spirit, and ongoing spiritual renewal and
refreshment through companionship with God. This continual
drinking of the Spirit is the key to being an overcomer.

In Verse 7, God himself declares who will inherit the
blessings and benefits of the new heaven and the new earth. It
is those who faithfully persevere in their devotion to Christ
and prove to be overcomers. Those who do not have a personal
relationship with God to help them overcome sin and
ungodliness will be thrown into the fiery lake according to
Revelation 21:8.

Revelation 21:8-26

Verse 8 shows what will not be there, circumstances and sin.

Verses 9-26 describe the New Heaven and New Earth.

- The Bride- The Wife of the Lamb v.9
- Twelve Gates- v.12
- The Lord...The Lamb are its Temple v.22
- Nations will walk v.24-26
- No Night There v.25

5

Epilogue:
Revelation 22

Revelation 22:1-6

These six verses give more characteristics of the New Heavens and the New Earth.

- River of Life v.1
- Tree of Life v.2
- No more curse v.3
- Seeing the Face of God, and Name in foreheads v.4
- No more Night in verse 5.

Revelation 22:7-21

In Verse 11, we see yet more canonical context to the book of Daniel, or more specifically Daniel 12:10 where it speaks about many will be purified but the wicked will continue to be wicked.

The first part of this passage is translated "the one being unrighteous let him be unrighteous still and the filthy one let him be filthy still" suggests several things to the hearers.

First of all, it could make one realize the possibility of hearing and taking heed to the prophecy, as the latter part of this passage shows by the lifestyle of being pure and holy. However, the ones mentioned in the first part of the text will not take heed but continue in their sins and disobedience. To see this may make one think of the Ezekiel 3:27 passage where it speaks of a rebellious house.

Second, the reader could think of encouragement for enduring such evil and his people, because of the second part of the verse shows a lifestyle of how to overcome the first portion of this verse.

Third, one could read this text and see how there is a need for repentance and how the time for that repentance is short with what is said in the verse before.[100]

There is also a grammatical word, in the Greek, that is a constant here and that is the word *e;ti*. Four times in this verse this word for "still" is mentioned, which suggests several things to me. First, the actions of this verse were a past event, but it is still ongoing. Second, that the events that precede this phrase will happen and continue to happen until the prophecy of the Apocalypse will be fulfilled.

Verse 12 begins with a prophetic promise by Christ himself. The phrase is translated "Indeed I am coming soon." This phrase, along with the declaration "my reward is with me", suggests a loose connection with Isaiah 40:10 in the LXX translation, which talks about the reward is with him and the Lord coming with strength.

The second phrase used here is "to repay each in proportion to his or her behavior". This brings to mind an allusion to Proverbs 24:12. In that passage, reference is made

---

[100] Christopher A. Davis: *Revelation: The College Press NIV Commentary Series: Electronic Edition,* (Joplin, College Press Publications, 2000) Libronix Scholars Library: Accessed November 17, 2007

to repaying for behavior.[101] This repayment is alluded to the previous verse in which some will be repaid for living right while others are not.

The whole verse, in context, can provide several meanings to the hearers. First, there is the fact that the exalted Christ functions as the judge here. Second, we will have a reward of some kind, but it is dependent on how we lived on earth based on the previous verses. Third, this is an overarching theme of the Epilogue in that not only is the time near for wrath, but it is also near for reward.

In Verse 13, we come to the authority in which Christ announces his coming and gives sentence to His judgment. The verse, which is translated, "I am Alpha and Omega the Beginning and the End" shows this authority.

This statement appears in two other passages in the Greek New Testament. It is found in Revelation 1:8 and in 21:6. These verses show this to be a divine title of the Father, but divine title of the Son as well.

This phrase could remind us of several things:

- First, Christ stands at the beginning of time and all creatures of time (John 1:1-3, Colossians 1:15-18, and Hebrews 1:10-14).
- Second, He stands at the end of all history folding up the heavens and the earth as one would fold a garment (Hebrews 1:11-12 and Psalm 102:25-27).
- Third, He stands as the Judge with absolute righteousness and equity (Isaiah 11:3-4).

The Alpha and Omega can also imply the following. First, is that fact that every soul has lived and died in His presence. Second, that not only is this an announcement of

---

[101] David E. Aune: *World Biblical Commentary Volume 52C: Revelation 17-22 Electronic Edition* (Dallas, Word Incorporated, 2002) S. 1217; Libronix Scholars Library Accessed November 17, 2007

his presence but also his sovereignty as well as it relates to the verses before this one.[102]

In Verse 14, we come to the last of the Seven Beatitudes in Revelation which is translated "blessed are the ones washing their robes." The term blessed here should make the reader think of the other times this terminology is used in Revelation 1:3, 14:3, 16:15, 19:9, 20:6, and 22:7.

This text brings us to the conclusion of the Judgment of the Lamb. It also concludes temporal blessings, as well, in that now the believer will experience eternal blessings.

In the manuscripts that surpass the King James Version of the text, one can see that those who wash their robes is translated "that do his commandments."

It is interesting to note that those who are blessed in this beatitude are to have access to the new Jerusalem and the Tree of Life. This shows how the text blends together as it describes the rewards Christ mentioned in the previous verses and throughout the book of Revelation to the Seven Churches and to the Redeemed.[103]

In Verse 15, we come to the contrast to verse 14. This describes those who will not be blessed, but rather those who are outside.

The term here, in the Greek, is in its verbal construction and always tends to be used after the verbs going, sending, placing, leading, drawing, etc., which commonly take prepositions or adverbs signifying rest in a place rather than those expressive of motion toward a place. This construction of this adjective, in this context, is to show the reader this is

---

[102] R. Hollis Gause: *Revelation: God's Stamp of Sovereignty on History* (Cleveland, Pathway, 1998) 281

[103] John F. Walvoord and Roy B. Zuck: *The Bible Knowledge Commentary: An Exposition of the Scriptures: Electronic Edition* (Wheaton, Victor Books, 1985) Libronix Scholars Library: Accessed November 18, 2007

the final outside destination.[104]

Those who were blessed were getting their reward while those who are outside were getting their judgment. This theme of contrast reminds the reader of a Canonical context that is found in the Old Testament of blessing and curses such as when Israel received instructions on the Law in the Pentateuch to the dedication of the Temple of Solomon in Second Chronicles.

In the New Testament, we see this function throughout the rest of the Apocalypse, and it would once again remind the reader of the Seven Churches account where there was a blessing and judgment to the hearers of the letters. This description is also in connection with an earlier description in the Apocalypse of the unsaved in Revelation 21:8,27.[105]

This brings emphasis to the fact that there is a final ending of the text, where the rewards mentioned in Revelation 2-3 are now being realized along with the warnings as well.

Verse 16 consists of two parts. The first part is translated, "I, Jesus, have sent my angel this message to you for the benefit of the churches."

There becomes an exegetical problem in this text with the term which is translated "you". This gets further complicated with the expression of the churches. The struggle lies upon to which churches this is referring.

The complication in the Greek text comes from the preposition before the term churches. This preposition brings the assumptions of either persons benefiting by an event, marking an experience by the event, or concerns of persons

[104] Joseph Henry Thayer: *A Greek-English Lexicon of the New Testament: Electronic Edition* (International Bible Translators, 2000) Bibleworks 7: Accessed November 18, 2007

[105] John F. Walvoord and Roy B. Zuck: *The Bible Knowledge Commentary: An Exposition of the Scriptures: Electronic Edition* (Wheaton, Victor Books, 1985) Libronix Scholars Library: Accessed November 18, 2007

from the event. These possible assumptions can complicate the churches context.[106]

Several theories lie in this phrase "the churches". First, many commentators take the term *u`mi/n* to refer to members of the Seven Churches in Revelation 2-3. The basis of this argument lies in the prologue in Revelation 1:4, where the introduction refers to the Seven Churches. The second argument for this exists in that the term is to mean a circle of Christian prophets, whose mission was to transmit the Revelation message to the churches. The third argument can be seen in that the application could be "you" as being the Christians individually, and the term churches being Christians collectively. The fourth argument is derived and modified from the third in that the "you" are the seven churches, and the churches is the rest of the Body of Christ. This duality of with one and the other is a theme throughout the Apocalypse which is seen in Revelation 22:9 where John is spoken about as a brother, prophet, and among those who obey the prophecy. Not only is he called a prophet but is a prophet. This theme is carried in the fact that Jesus was not a prophet but here brings prophecy.[107]

In the second part of verse 16 we come to another name Christ uses to identify himself with the reader. This phrase is translated "I am David's descendent the Bright and Morning Star", which signifies yet another canonical context.

The reader can see several implications here on the "I am" statement. First of all, the reader immediately thinks of the other instances, in the Apocalypse, where this terminology is

[106] David E. Aune: *The Prophetic Circle of John of Patmos and the Exegesis of Revelation 22:16*, Journal for the Study of the New Testament (October 1989): 103-116. ATLA Religion Database with ATLASerials, EBSCOhost (Accessed November 6, 2007).

[107] David E. Aune: *World Biblical Commentary Volume 52C: Revelation 17-22 Electronic Edition* (Dallas, Word Incorporated, 2002) S. 1217; Libronix Scholars Library Accessed November 17, 2007

used (1:8, 17, 2:23, 21:6). Second, this could also make the reader reflect to the Old Testament and the story of Moses, in which God appears to him in Exodus and states "I am". Third, this text could take the reader back to the fourth Gospel to be reminded of the "I am" sayings of Jesus in that text as well.

The phrase here for the Root and the Offspring of David can be canonically contextual to the Isaiah 1:10 passage in the Old Testament and the Apocalypse's earlier account in 5:5.

The terminology Bright and Morning Star can be linked to Numbers 24:17 and Isaiah 60:3.[108] As the Bright and Morning Star, He introduces the day of the Lord. He is the light shining in a dark place, and he is the Daystar rising in the hearts of the believers.[109] The relationship of the two terms ties in the Old and New Testament references of Joel and 2 Peter.

In Verse 17, we come to a prophetic cry. In the first part of this passage we "And the Spirit and the Bride say Come." In the Structure of Revelation, we know the Spirit plays a huge part in it, with four "In the Spirit" notations. However, in this text, we see just the term *pneu/ma.* This alone has another sighting in Revelation 14:13. In this first part we also come to the term "the bride." We must understand, the Bride in this context cannot possibly mean the seven churches mentioned in Revelation 2-3, as this bride is pure while several of these churches were warned about their impurity. Another comparison would be that the seven churches were unprepared for the coming of Christ, especially Ephesus, Pergamum, and Thyatira verses the desperation of the Bride here in Revelation chapter 22. With these two comparisons, we can clearly see

---

[108] David E. Aune: *World Biblical Commentary Volume 52C: Revelation 17-22 Electronic Edition* (Dallas, Word Incorporated, 2002) S. 1217; Libronix Scholars Library Accessed November 17, 2007

[109] R. Hollis Gause: *Revelation: God's Stamp of Sovereignty on History* (Cleveland, Pathway, 1998) 283

the church at end of Revelation is Spirit led and cries for the coming of Christ.[110]

The second part of Verse 17 deals with the phrase "And who is hearing come and who is thirsty come and take the water of life without cost." This term here water of life deals with the invitation to salvation before the first part of the phrase is fulfilled. The canonical context of this verse can be seen in John 7:37-39 where the invitation is given here also to come and drink.[111]

The fourth gospel account ties in once again with the Spirit, because after the invitation in the John's gospel is given, there are the rivers of living water reference which is attributed to the outpouring of the Spirit. This text shows a total connection of the Spirit, not just in the Church or being led by the Spirit, but the Church receiving the Spirit as well.

Verse 18 begins a two-fold warning in tampering with the prophecy of the Apocalypse. "If anyone adds to the prophecy, God will add the plagues described in this book" is an extraordinarily strong prophetic warning. This warning could mean several things.

First, it could mean to assure accuracy of the prophecy. According to Jewish tradition, this gave scribes an added importance to copy their works carefully. Along with this fact, is the reality that this warning was particularly characteristic of the Jews in their view of the inviolate nature of Scripture (Deuteronomy 4:2, 12:32).

Second, this warning could convey an assurance of an obedience to commands. This could have served as a reminder to the reader to keep the commands given as John spoke about

---

[110] Richard Bauckham, *The Climax of Prophecy: Studies in the Book of Revelation,* (London, T and T Clark, 2000), 35, 167

[111] John F. Walvoord and Roy B. Zuck: *The Bible Knowledge Commentary: An Exposition of the Scriptures: Electronic Edition* (Wheaton, Victor Books, 1985) Libronix Scholars Library: Accessed November 18, 2007

in Revelation 1:3.

Third, a look at the condition of the churches of Asia would show the reader that a threat to add to the prophecy. This could be particularly relevant in the fact that we have a false prophet amid one of the seven churches in 2:20.[112]

Verse 19 completes this warning by using the opposite of verse 18 with the phrase which is translated "if anyone takes away from the book". Some scholars claim that this warning expands also to the setting and purpose of each Biblical passage. However, in the context of this verse, it is clear in the Greek and English translations that it means "this prophecy" in terms of the Apocalypse only.

The result of taking away is different from adding to, in that if you take away you basically lose your reward as a believer which is found in the previous verses concerning the tree of life and the heavenly city. One of the best ways to avoid any of the above some scholars say is to swallow the book whole. I have found too this to be the case.[113]

Verse 20 shows a dialogue between Jesus and the writer. There are three parts to this verse.

The first part lies in the phrase which is translated "He who testifies to this." This is no doubt Jesus, not just in the fact because in the second part he is identified but also the use of "testify" is similar to the use of the term for witness in Revelation 1:5 and 3:14.

The second part to this verse is translated "surely I am coming soon". The term here is often, in the Greek grammar,

---

[112] Robert L. Thomas: "The Spiritual Gift of Prophecy in Revelation 22:18", *Journal of the Evangelical Theological Society* Volume 32 Number 2 (June 1989), 201-216, ATLA Religion Database with ATLASerials, EBSCOhost (Accessed November 6, 2007).

[113] Robert M. Royalty: "Don't Touch This Book: Revelation 22:18-19 and the Rhetoric of Reading in the Apocalypse of John." *Biblical Interpretation Volume 12 Number 3 (2004) 282-299* ATLA Religion Database with ATLASerials, EBSCOhost (Accessed November 6, 2007).

a synonym with giving the reader a particle of affirmation with solemn assurance of the truth of the statement that is following. It is interesting to point out this is the second time in the epilogue that Jesus says He is coming, giving yet an emphasis on His return. This phrase can be found in five different reference in the prophetic present in Revelation including passages such as 2:16, 3:11, 22:7, 12, and here in verse 20.

In the third part of this passage is "Amen come Lord Jesus." When the reader looks at this one could easily mistake this for a prayer. However, this is not the case. In the text it is seen as a part of the dialogue in which this statement was a response to the previous statement. This term for "come" is a present imperative which is a rarity in New Testament Greek. The present imperative gives the reader insight that John was agreeing with Jesus' statement.

There are three questions to ask ourselves here about this verse. The first is "does this refer to the cultic coming of Jesus?" The second is "does this refer to the eschatological coming of Jesus?" The third is "could it be both cultic and eschatological?"

It is safe to say that the second plays better than one or three in the questions raised here.[114] In looking at the text it obviously deals with a second coming, because he is still at the right hand of the Father in heaven. To say it is a coming already taken place would try to put the Apocalypse in chronological order which is impossible to do because Revelation is a circular book. For example, it causes a fall out in the book, as a whole, because what do you do with the judgments and wrath of the Lamb, along with issues such as

---

[114] David E. Aune: *World Biblical Commentary Volume 52C: Revelation 17-22 Electronic Edition* (Dallas, Word Incorporated, 2002) S. 1217; Libronix Scholars Library Accessed November 17, 2007

the Two witnesses who are attacked by the beast in Rev. 11 but the beast doesn't show up until 13? These challenges make it hard to even attempt to put Revelation in order. It is with this that an eschatological coming of Jesus is a must in the interpretation of this verse.

Verse 21 gives a benediction of "the grace of the Lord Jesus Christ be with you all." John follows suit here canonically with using a standard farewell, as seen in the other Epistles of the New Testament. Does this make Revelation an epistle? No, it is just a concluding remark to an eschatological reality that Christ is soon to return.

BIBLIOGRAPHY

Aune, David E.: *World Biblical Commentary Volume 52C: Revelation 17-22 Electronic Edition* (Dallas, Word Incorporated, 2002) S. 1217; Libronix Scholars Library Accessed November 17, 2007

Aune, David E. "The prophetic circle of John of Patmos and the exegesis of Revelation 22:16." *Journal for the Study of the New Testament* (October 1989): 103-116. *ATLA Religion Database with ATLASerials*, EBSCO*host;* Accessed November 20, 2007

Bauckham, Richard, *The Climax of Prophecy: Studies in the Book of Revelation,* London, T and T Clark, 2000

Bozorghmehr, Shirzad: Annan: 'Dismay' over Iranian comments on Israel', CNN.COM, http://www.cnn.com/2005/WORLD/meast/10/27/ahmadinejad.reaction/, Accessed: April 14, 2008

Bread for the World Website: http://www.bread.org/learn/hunger-basics/, Accessed: April 14, 2008

Cohen, Gary G.: *Revelation Visualized*: (Chattanooga, AMG, 1981)

Collins, Adela Yarbro: "Revelation": *The Anchor Bible Dictionary: David Noel Freedman, Editor: Electronic*

Edition, New York, Doubleday, 1996, 5:693 Libronix Scholars' Library (accessed November 18, 2007)

Davis, Christopher A.: *Revelation: The College Press NIV Commentary Series: Electronic Edition,* Joplin, College Press Publications, 2000, Libronix Scholars Library: Accessed November 17, 2007

Easton, Matthew George : *Easton's Illustrated Bible Dictionary: Electronic Edition*: (Ephihamy Software, 1995)

Gause, R. Hollis: *Revelation: God's Stamp of Sovereignty on History* Cleveland, Pathway, 1998

Hughes, Robert B. ; Laney, J. Carl ; Hughes, Robert B.: *Tyndale Concise Bible Commentary*: (Wheaton, Tyndale House Publishers, 2001)

Jamieson, Robert ; Fausset, A. R. ; Fausset, A. R. ; Brown, David ; Brown, David: *A Commentary, Critical and Explanatory, on the Old and New Testaments*: (Oak Harbor, Logos Research Systems, Inc., 1997)

Koester, Craig R., *Revelation and the End of All Things,* Grand Rapids, Eerdmans, 2001

McGee, J. Vernon : *Thru the Bible with J. Vernon McGee*: (Nashville, Thomas Nelson, 1983)

Royalty, Robert M. "Don't touch this book!: Revelation 22:18-19 and the rhetoric of reading (in) the Apocalypse of John." *Biblical Interpretation* 12, no. 3 (2004): 282-299. *ATLA Religion Database with ATLASerials*, EBSCO*host* Accessed November 20, 2007

Strong, James: *Strong's Concordance*: (Austin, WORDsearch, 2007).

Thayer, Joseph Henry: *A Greek-English Lexicon of the New Testament: Electronic Edition* International Bible Translators, 2000, Bibleworks 7: Accessed November 18, 2007

Thomas, John Christopher. Two Horizons Commentary: Revelation. Grand Rapids, Michigan: Wm. B. Eerdmans Publishing Company, 2016.

Thomas, Robert L. "The spiritual gift of prophecy in Rev 22:18." *Journal of the Evangelical Theological Society* 32, no. 2 (June 1989): 201-216. *ATLA Religion Database with ATLASerials*, EBSCO*host*, Accessed November 20, 2007

Voorhis, G.D.: *Satan Exposed:* (Asheboro, Village Printing, 1973)

_____ *Questions and Answers in the Book of Revelation:* (Asheboro, Village Printing, 1988)

_____ *The Course of This Present Age:* (Asheboro, Village Printing, 1974)

Waddell, Robby: *The Spirit of the Book of Revelation*: (Blandford Forum, Deo, 2006)

Walvoord, John F. and Zuck, Roy B.: *The Bible Knowledge Commentary: An Exposition of the Scriptures: Electronic Edition,* Wheaton, Victor Books, 1985; Libronix Scholars Library: (accessed November 18, 2007)

Wiersbe, Warren W.: *The Bible Exposition Commentary*: (Wheaton, Victor Books, 1996)

Willmington, H. L.: *Willmington's Bible Handbook*: (Wheaton, Tyndale House Publishers, 1997)

_____: *The Outline Bible*: (Wheaton, Tyndale House Publishers, 1999)

OutFlow

Publishing

Valdese, North Carolina

Made in the USA
Columbia, SC
16 October 2021

46952995R00090